Dyslexia and Me

How to Survive and Thrive if You're Neurodivergent

Onyinye Udokporo

Jessica Kingsley Publishers
London and Philadelphia

First published in Great Britain in 2023 by Jessica Kingsley Publishers
An imprint of Hodder & Stoughton Ltd
An Hachette Company

1

Copyright © Onyinye Udokporo 2023

Front cover image source: Jovilee Burton.

The fonts, layout and overall design of this book have been prepared according to dyslexia-friendly principles. At JKP we aim to make our books' content accessible to as many readers as possible.

A CIP catalogue record for this title is available from the British Library and the Library of Congress

ISBN 978 1 78775 944 2
eISBN 978 1 78775 945 9

Printed and bound in Great Britain by TJ Books Limited

Jessica Kingsley Publishers' policy is to use papers that are natural, renewable and recyclable products and made from wood grown in sustainable forests. The logging and manufacturing processes are expected to conform to the environmental regulations of the country of origin.

Jessica Kingsley Publishers
Carmelite House
50 Victoria Embankment
London EC4Y 0DZ

www.jkp.com

"'You can't be what you can't see', was perhaps Onyinye's biggest barrier in life. This book shows how this barrier, present in other people's minds and the systems they created were overcome. Onyinye's resilience and neurodivergent strengths, and her parents and others that valued her for those gifts, allowed her to smash those barriers and with this book and her enterprise help many others who still to this day face the same. With our focus on accessibility in our technology, to empower every person to achieve more, it is truly rewarding to see how this underpinned Onyinye's strength to allow her to be her true best self and light the path for others so that they can see hope and a future."

– *Michael Vermeersch, Accessibility Product Marketing Manager, Microsoft*

"This book is enriched with so many golden nuggets and tips and it highlights for me why representation matters. It is so important to be able to see ourselves in books, when talking about self-identity, a sense of belonging and breaking barriers of stigma of dyslexia from a cultural perspective. I wish I had a book like this in my teens as a young black girl, to inspire me. A common theme throughout the book is about navigating the education system and the importance of support from family, friends and educators. In my 30 years working as an educator, cultural literacy is missing from the table in our schools and university libraries. Books like this need to be embedded in our education system towards true inclusion as well as adding diversity into neurodiversity."

– *Marcia Brissett-Bailey, Top 50 Influential Neurodivergent Women 2022, author, dyslexic, neurodiversity advocate and champion, Observer of the BDA Executive Board and co-founder of the BDA Cultural Perspective Committee (Chair)*

"I thoroughly enjoyed reading this open, honest and personal account of dyslexia at different ages and levels of education. I related to many of the strategies and advice suggested. I think this book captures the importance of inclusivity and diverse role models for anyone with dyslexia."

– *Alais Winton, author of* Fun Games and Activities for Children with Dyslexia of related interest

The Adult Side of Dyslexia
Kelli Sandman-Hurley
ISBN 978 1 78775 475 1
eISBN 978 1 78775 476 8

**The Bigger Picture Book of Amazing
Dyslexics and the Jobs They Do**
Kathy Iwanczak Forsyth and Kate Power
Foreword by Paul Smith
ISBN 978 1 78592 584 9
eISBN 978 1 78592 585 6

Creative, Successful, Dyslexic
23 High Achievers Share Their Stories
Margaret Rooke
Foreword by Mollie King
ISBN 978 1 84905 653 3
eISBN 978 1 78450 163 1

Fun Games and Activities for Children with Dyslexia
How to Learn Smarter with a Dyslexic Brain
Alais Winton
ISBN 978 1 78592 292 3
eISBN 978 1 78450 596 7

**The Memory and Processing
Guide for Neurodiverse Learners**
Strategies for Success
Alison Patrick
ISBN 978 1 78775 072 2
eISBN 978 1 78775 073 9

Contents

Preface   7

Chapter 1   13

Spell Soap...S–O–O–P

Chapter 2   37

Colour, Creed and Circumstance

Chapter 3   51

En Route to British Boarding School

Chapter 4   71

Secondary Education...Struggles and Solutions

Chapter 5   99

Building Enrich Learning

Chapter 6   113
#FFE312

Chapter 7   143
From Kensington Olympia to London Waterloo

Chapter 8   177
The BA to MA Transition

Epilogue   195

Resources   197

Index   203

Preface

I'm going to start this book by introducing myself, because having an understanding of the woman I have become today will help you to make sense of my story. My name is Onyinyewchukwu Jakirichi Ekpereamaka Chiatuogo Udokporo, MA – but you can call me Onyinye (pronounced: O-nin-yay). I'm from London and I'm of Nigerian (Igbo) heritage.

By the age of 22 I had completed two degrees. My undergraduate degree is in Religion, Politics and Society and my postgraduate degree is in Education, Policy and Society. Both degrees are from King's College London where I received the first ever Student of the Year award, and I was named as one of the top 10 Black Students in the UK by Rare Recruitment, sponsored by the Universities of Cambridge and Oxford.[1]

Aged 12 I started a tutoring business, and have since built it into an online tuition platform and EdTech software distributor known as **Enrich Learning**. I was inspired to start the business following my successful attempt, through studying really hard myself, at taking various 11+ exams, which granted me a place at the leading charitable school, Christ's Hospital.[2]

I'm an entrepreneur, education expert, factual TV presenter, writer and pioneer of social mobility. I'm deeply passionate about creating greater access to opportunity using education as a tool to level the playing field. As well as all the above, I'm a proud, black, dyslexic woman.

I was diagnosed with dyslexia aged 11. I have always found reading, writing and spelling challenging. I don't come from a background where neurodivergence and learning differences are openly discussed. My saving grace was the fact that my parents have always had an open mind.

I found my primary school years quite hard. While in many ways I did well academically, every school report came with a "but" that was almost always linked to my inability to read, write and spell properly. I enjoyed studying, but it exhausted me in a way that my fellow peers could not relate to. It was especially obvious when I did homework with my three brothers.

Kachi, who is only 13 months younger than me, would fly through his homework tasks. The letters of the words for our weekly spelling tests effortlessly rolled off his tongue while I anxiously stood next to him, with beads of sweat trickling down the sides of my face as I tried to keep up. As the eldest child at home, I found homework both tiresome and embarrassing. At the time, academia for me was always accompanied with what felt like a permanent struggle. I am fortunate to have parents who did and who continue to do everything they can to support me, even if they're not quite sure what the problem is.

Despite being members of a community that considers learning differences and neurodivergence to be taboo topics (which I say more about later in this book), my mum and dad strived to educate themselves on these matters, and in doing so, empowered me to believe that dyslexia is one of my many gifts. I built courage from seeing my parents positively embrace my dyslexia diagnosis.

My mum is especially vocal about it. I recall hearing her on the phone to other mums using my dyslexia story to encourage and uplift them. My story became a beacon of hope for members of the community that I am from. This book is my attempt to inspire and educate readers about the beauty of neurodivergence. I will also tell you about the pitfalls I have experienced with dyslexia, and will share the tips I created and used to overcome them.

Before I go any further, it is important that you understand why I have written this book. Throughout my life I have been told, directly and indirectly, that dyslexia is found in particular people. At the beginning of my dyslexic journey, I was shown successful, middle-aged, white men who were so far removed from my world, but who happened to be dyslexic. I was expected to relate to them and to use them as a source of inspiration. The problem was that, at 11 years old, I simply could not see how Richard Branson, Jamie Oliver and Albert Einstein were like me. Giving me such examples limited my mindset – at that time I had no interest in becoming a business magnate, a chef or a deceased scientist. I just wanted to be shown that dyslexia can be found in someone like me, and that it wasn't just "okay" but something to be proud of.

I wrote this book because I want people to know that dyslexia can be found in people of every colour, creed or circumstance. Dyslexia can be found in every community, culture and social class. Being dyslexic and, more generally, being neurodivergent, is not taboo. With dyslexia I have been able to achieve more than anyone could have ever predicted. In telling my story, I hope to inspire and encourage you. Dyslexia is something to be embraced. It is often seen as a burden when in actual fact it is something of a blessing that comes with so many gifts. You simply have to learn **how** to uncover those gifts, and it just so happens that this book is my attempt to teach you that.

Notes

1. www.kcl.ac.uk/news/kings-student-named-uks-top-ten-black-university-students

2. Christ's Hospital is a remarkable school; it is the UK's leading charitable school and largest bursary charity. The school was established in 1552 and provides free or substantially reduced cost places to over 630 of its 900 pupils each year – this is more than any other organization in the UK.

Chapter 1

Spell Soap...S–O–O–P

I want to take you with me on a trip down memory lane. This is a flashback to when I was five years old. It's the early evening and I'm nervously standing next to my younger brother as we prepare for our weekly spelling recital, commonly known as a spelling bee. This wasn't anything official, just a makeshift version my parents created to help us get ready for our school's weekly spelling tests.

I can still remember the feeling of saliva clogging my throat as I tried to recall the words in my head before my performance. I can see my parents sitting up in bed, my dad holding the list of words in his hands, with the sheet of paper placed between his nose and eyebrows. I could only see the slits of his watchful eyes as he raised his head above the page, a signal that the spelling bee was about to begin. My mum sat beside my dad and gave me a somewhat confident smile. I remember feeling a sense of doubt coming from her, but it wasn't strong enough to discourage me. Dad cleared his throat, and said:

Spell "soap".

My thoughts raced ahead of the letters that left my mouth. I confidently spoke the letters: "S–O–O–P". Both my parents looked at each other and appeared to be in a state of shock. I thought I'd hit the jackpot and smiled. My dad then repeated himself, raising his voice slightly and maintaining a rather stern tone:

Onyinyewchukwu, spell "soap".

I spoke again, this time with so much confidence it was borderline audacious.

S–O–O–P.

My dad let out a sad sigh and my mum's head hung low. My dad then turned to my younger brother and said, "Son, spell 'soap'."

My brother smiled and reeled off his version effortlessly:

S−O−A−P.

My brother stood there calm and collected while I stood there asking myself, "Why did Daddy call me by my full name?" My full first name was only used when I had done something wrong. Little did I know that I had, in fact, done something wrong – I had spelt "soap" incorrectly and my brother, 13 months my junior, had beat me to it...again.

My dad gleamed and said, "That's my boy", quickly followed by "Onyinye, how could you spell 'soap' incorrectly?" My dad wasn't angry, but his facial expression was one of deep disappointment. It goes without saying that disappointment from your parent is worse than anger. My parents could not understand how I could not spell the simplest of words. At the age of five, and in full-time education,

I was expected to be able to spell basic words with ease.

To some extent, this expectation made sense. My mum had spent a lot of time with me earlier that week, practising for our family spelling bee. I was also having weekly private tuition classes. The focus of these classes was spelling, reading and writing. I had rehearsed and practised the list for that week's test in what should have been my playtimes. Given all the extra time, effort and resources that were being poured into my academic studies, to my parents and me there was no legitimate explanation as to why I could not spell the word "soap".

I don't recall being a disobedient child, but I was at my wits end with the spelling bee that day. It was one of the few times in my childhood where I turned my back on my parents and walked away. Tears silently streamed down my face as I internally questioned what was wrong with me. I could hear my brother eagerly pressing ahead with the list of words. He even knew when to pause for dramatic effect, making the audience (my parents) believe he was about to fail to spell a word correctly. Of course, my brother's pauses were only ever for dramatic effect. He never put a foot wrong. As he celebrated his inevitable success, my mum crept out of the room and stretched her hands out, inviting me for a hug.

Then something extraordinary happened. My mum took me to one side and whispered in my ear that she couldn't spell either. I remember looking up at her and thinking that no one's spelling could be worse than mine. She went on to explain that, like me, she was the eldest child with a brother whose academic excellence always outshone hers. Like me, she failed to pass the weekly spelling tests and her brother's spelling success became the norm in their home. Her parents tried as much as they could to help her with her spelling, but it was a skill she struggled to develop.

When my mum was a child, she had not known that she was dyslexic, and this is why she had struggled at school. She had grown up at a time when learning differences were not known about. And she had also grown up in a place where people didn't believe in learning differences. My mum explicitly remembered her father's concern regarding her inability to spell proficiently and her challenges with reading well. At the time there were very few resources to help him understand my mum's struggle. This doesn't mean he wasn't supportive of her, though – my mother was a successful entrepreneur, and his support was a vital part of her success. However, he did not push her academically as he didn't want to cause her undue stress. While my mum now appreciates the sentiment behind his thinking, she was (and still is) of the view that education is essential in order to succeed. So she wasn't going to mollycoddle me; instead she pledged to investigate this issue further.

Part of her investigation led us to discover that dyslexia is genetic. The National Health Service reports that the exact cause of dyslexia is unknown, but it often runs in families. It is thought that certain genes inherited from parents may act together in a way that affects how some parts of the brain develop during early life. It is not uncommon for a child with dyslexia to have an immediate family member who also has this learning difference. It is also not unusual for multiple children in a family to have dyslexia. Despite dyslexia being genetic in its origin, there has been no discovery of a "dyslexia gene". Dyslexia is associated with over 40 genes, and these do a lot of different things. It is widely recognized that more time and money needs to be spent on dyslexia research, and there is still so much to discover.

Having studied biology until I left school aged 17 (I'm an August baby, so very young for my school year), I find the science behind dyslexia rather interesting. So I want to use this as an opportunity to dispel the scientific myths about dyslexia that I have been told over the years.

It is important to understand that both mothers and fathers can pass dyslexia on to their child/ren if either parent has it. I mention this specific fact because there are a few genes that are associated with dyslexia on the X chromosome. This has led to the development of the myth that you're likely to get dyslexia from your mother, as women have two X chromosomes, while men have one X chromosome and one Y chromosome. This myth has meant that some women have been blamed for "giving their child or children dyslexia". This simply isn't the case. In actual fact, more boys are diagnosed with dyslexia than girls. It is important that the scientific facts about dyslexia are known because they support my belief, which is that **anyone** can be dyslexic.

My mum assured me that she was going to get to the bottom of my spelling problem. She was determined to stop history repeating itself. After all, I was born in London where there was supposedly greater access to opportunity. In Northern Nigeria, my mum's birthplace, a child who could not spell was labelled as "dumb". My mum made me know that in the UK attitudes were different – although it's fair to say that, at the time, the difference was not significant enough for the UK to be praised for its treatment of neurodivergent people. There will be more on this later on in this chapter.

Mum and I spoke at length about my spelling problems. We laughed and we cried. I remember telling my mum that I was desperate to improve. I had all the will in the world because I was fed up with feeling hopeless – even at five years old. We devised a rather daring plan. My mum committed to daily 60-word spelling tests. Every night, she sat with the dictionary and picked words that she felt I would need to know as a primary school student. She bought a notebook, which famously became known as "the spelling book". Every morning, I would sit at the table and my mum and I would do the 60-word spelling test. It was difficult, to begin with. Even now, I do wonder why I never gave up because there were days where I'd have been lucky to achieve a score above 5 out of 60. I do know that my persistence to carry on with these tiresome spelling tests was linked to this idea that if I could spell, I could do anything.

Each week I got better, the scores got higher, and the bond with my mum grew stronger. There were times when my mum and I would do these spelling tests at the crack of dawn. My dad would walk past the front room and give me a smile of encouragement. I'm sure he thought my desire to spell had become obsessive but, because I was a daddy's girl, he supported everything I wanted to do – even if he thought it was crazy. I began to get top marks in these tests. On a few occasions,

I achieved a higher score than my brother – that was especially satisfying.

My mum and I noticed that I had a secret weapon that aided me in these tests. If I spent enough time writing out and looking at the words, I remembered them with ease. I never practised **how** to spell these words; I took a mental snapshot of them. During the spelling tests, I would shut my eyes and the words would appear. Unknown to my mum and I at the time, I had something of a photographic memory.

I began to use this superpower in other aspects of my life. Both of my parents were (and still are) pretty bad at remembering directions. While I'm hopeless at reading a map, I am like a human satnav. I developed a bespoke mental Google Maps that got my family from one destination to the next seamlessly. My brain would retain basic journeys right through to escapades that took us across the M25. I also became the household safe in the sense that all the important pins and passwords became my responsibility because I never seemed to forget them. Again, all I would do to recall this information was close my eyes and a vivid image would appear.

On reflection, I can now see that I never really learnt how to spell. Instead, I spent hours memorizing mnemonics. My favourite was the mnemonic for the word "necessary": "**n**ever **e**at **c**hocolate, **e**at **s**ummer fruits **s**alad **a**nd **r**emain **y**oung". I still use this method to spell correctly. I crammed all the words my mum believed that I needed to know as a primary school student. This was also when my photographic memory came to light, a gift from my neurodivergence that most people don't have. It is believed that between 2 and 10% of children have photographic memories.[1]

After some extensive research, we discovered that not only did I have a photographic memory, but I also had an eidetic memory, something that's similar, but not the same. An eidetic memory is the ability to vividly recall an image you are exposed to, but only briefly (for example, someone may be able to continue to "see" a picture they have been shown for 30 seconds, even a few minutes after the picture is removed).[2] Having an eidetic memory is one of the factors that is analysed when a child has been diagnosed with dyslexia.[3] It is believed that the eidetic memory is used for unusual words with unlikely spellings, such as "laugh", "said", "yacht" and "tongue".[4] In other words, dyslexic children tend to cram the words that do not sound anything like the way they are spelt. I can admit to spending days looking at and re-writing these types of words for hours on end in a bid to learn how they were spelt so I would pass the spelling tests. I used the gift of an eidetic memory to mask my dyslexia.

Having my spelling under control was one thing; getting my written work to make coherent sense was another. While I was able to work my way to the top in the school spelling tests, I still struggled to write well. I was creative and would often re-write Jacqueline Wilson's storylines with my own twist; however, my sentences were so long they would take you days to complete reading. My work was poorly punctuated, and my thoughts scattered over several pages. There was no structure to my writing.

I was made aware of my insufficient writing skills at my Year 3 (age 7–8) parents' evening. I sat sandwiched between my parents facing my teacher, Mrs Johnson. I remember Mrs Johnson distinctly because she was the first black teacher I'd ever had.

She told us that she had recently come from Jamaica. She had a thick Caribbean accent and would often switch between speaking English and Jamaican Patois. She was tall, with a slim frame, and always wore her hair in a thick, curly, black afro to school. Mrs Johnson had a pile of my work in front of her, as well as my class workbook. She smiled and welcomed my parents and I remember feeling excited that my parents would be able to see what I was working on in school. We exchanged greetings, and then Mrs Johnson quickly dived into the business of the day – my poorly written English work.

My class workbook had red pen markings all over it, indicating where my sentences should have started and stopped. Mrs Johnson had scribbled over my immaculately presented written pieces, placing full stops and commas where they ought to have been. Halfway through the meeting, she stood up, marched over to the board, scribbled down the word **"and"**, and then put a massive red cross through it. It seems that I had overused that conjunction in my work. Somehow my eyes retained my tears and I smiled. I remember spending the entire parents' evening looking up to the sky, praying for a miracle that something positive would be said about me so that my parents wouldn't be disappointed again. After Mrs Johnson's rather damning monologue about my work, she suddenly exclaimed:

> "But Onyinye is clever, she tries very hard, and I want to help her!"

My parents looked at each other and drew their chairs into the table as they listened carefully to Mrs Johnson. Mrs Johnson admitted that she couldn't tell my parents what the root cause of my writing problems was. I was always well behaved and paid attention, so she couldn't say that my inability to express myself clearly on paper was due to bad behaviour. I had masked my inability to spell by cramming all the words – my scores in the weekly spelling tests were consistently high. This meant that she couldn't use my spelling to build a case that may have helped her realize I needed additional support from the special educational needs team.

She admitted that in her experience of teaching, she hadn't come across a student like me before.

She knew there was a problem, but wasn't sure on how to fix it or where to start. Simply put, Mrs Johnson had not been trained or even made aware of what learning differences were and how they might show up in the classroom. Nonetheless, she tried her very best. She scheduled one-to-one teaching time with me in break times. My writing improved with time, and by the end of the year, I had climbed to the very top of the class in English.

Before I go on to tell you more about my primary school years, I want to tell you about certain parts of my early school experience that, on reflection, are rather problematic. The first is that it amazes me that my class teacher had no training in spotting the signs of a child with learning differences. Mrs Johnson was able to identify that I was struggling despite my diligence and hard work, but she couldn't put her finger on the issue at hand. This led her to assume that if I worked harder, all would be well. While this has helped me develop an incredible work ethic, it also made me believe that I was to blame for my inability to read, write and spell properly. This bred an unhealthy habit of being my own inner critic and having a low opinion of myself, which I carried into my teenage years.

In 2014, the campaigning organization, the Driver Youth Trust, published *The Fish in the Tree: Why We Are Failing Children with Dyslexia*,[5] which stated that 52% of teachers surveyed received no training on dyslexia. It went on to state that 84% of teachers surveyed thought it was important that teachers were trained in teaching children with dyslexia. While there have been significant improvements in the classroom regarding the identification of dyslexia, with 63% of teachers feeling "somewhat" confident in their ability to identify it,[6] it's clear that more needs to be done to better equip teachers on how to teach neurodivergent children – those with dyslexia, dyspraxia and other different learning styles – in a classroom that is run for children who learn in a more conventional way.

The second part of my experience that I now take issue with is the fact that my parents, who were eager to find support for me, had nowhere to turn for guidance. When I look back, what stands out to me most is the real lack of community for parents in the dyslexic world. As an adult now, I have a greater understanding of how isolated my parents must have felt when trying to find support for me. Dyslexia, and neurodiversity more widely, are not topics that are readily up for discussion in many ethnic communities. In fact, I am going to unapologetically state that neurodivergence is considered taboo in many ethnic communities, and this book is my attempt to start a much-needed conversation to change this.

When I was a child, dyslexia-focused organizations such as the British Dyslexia Association (BDA) were in existence, but my parents did not contact them for a number of reasons. The first reason was that I had not been screened or assessed for dyslexia. Without confirmation that I was dyslexic, they had no reason to contact organizations that could support them. My parents and my teachers knew I faced challenges at school, especially when reading, writing and spelling, but they didn't know it was linked to a neurological condition. Like most parents from my community, my parents were careful about "labelling" any of their children. They especially would not want to have their eldest child, the leader of the pack, be "labelled" with any condition. Contacting the BDA would have increased the likelihood of me being "labelled". This was something my parents simply weren't ready for. While they are open minded and wanted to find a solution for me, being labelled with a condition that they knew nothing about was very much out of their comfort zone. Additionally, at the time they had to focus on managing the pressures of trying to raise four children to the best of their ability. They were time poor but also conscious of how me being "labelled" with dyslexia would reflect on them as parents. Being told that your child has a condition with no cure can be a hard pill to swallow for **any** parent. Avoidance is a coping mechanism. In this case my parents avoided the dyslexia label until they were in a position where they could fully engage with the problem. I know that many parents will initially have the same response if they suspect that their child is dyslexic too.

The hostility towards dyslexia and other learning differences in their culture and upbringing, caused by the lack of education around the topic of neurodiversity, meant that my parents had to find solutions to my problems privately and independently. This was not only expensive, it was also emotionally draining. My parents had no one to reassure them that the active steps they were taking would help me succeed in school. While I highly commend my parents for their efforts, and appreciate that they did everything they could to support me, I know that I would have achieved a lot more in my early primary school years if they had been able to access the **right** academic support for me. And I think it's fair to say that they would also have appreciated having an ear to listen to the different solutions that they developed for me.

Despite the challenges, my parents, Mrs Johnson and I pressed ahead with making sure I maximized my academic potential in the best way I could, although our resources were limited, and there was little to no funding for me at school. One of my classmate's parents volunteered to come in and read with me weekly, and my parents took turns in listening to me reading out loud. I fondly remember reading children's classics by Roald Dahl, Jacqueline Wilson and Meg Cabot while my mum cooked our dinner. The smell of jollof rice brings back fond memories of me sitting on a stool beside her, often reading with a raised voice as I competed with the sounds of sizzling onions and boiling tomatoes. My dad preferred a more "theatrical" performance, and would encourage me to read aloud to the family at any given opportunity.

While I cannot confirm whether these techniques helped improve my reading skills, they did build my confidence immensely. So, if I had to specify two things that helped me in my primary years – which might help you if you're dyslexic, or if you know someone who is – they were:

1. Continuous words of encouragement, positive affirmations and reassurance that I could read, spell and write, even when it seemed like I couldn't. These helped to build my self-esteem. With a healthy dose of self-esteem, you can do anything you put your mind to.

2. Help your child understand that reading is useful! Encourage and help them to read at every given opportunity. I read road signs, train station notices and billboards. I recommend

quite literally encouraging your child to read everything. This will help them see the point in learning to read a book. The more practice your child has, the less fearful they will be of reading in the long term. These ad hoc reading exercises also helped me build resilience. My parents did not allow me to be defeatist in my attitude towards my dyslexia, and this was an important lesson to learn at an early age. They rehearsed every word I struggled to pronounce with me, and even as an adult they still lend their ears to my many mispronunciations. They recognized the importance of empowering me to believe that I could do anything I put my mind to.

At a more practical level, there are now many more learning resources available online that are suited to dyslexic learners and their different brains. You can find details of these, and try them out to see what works for you, on the websites of organizations like the British Dyslexia Association[7] and International Dyslexia Association.[8] I also hope that books like mine will do something to tackle the stigma of dyslexia in some communities and cultures.

Notes

1. Searleman, A. (2007) 'Is there such a thing as a photographic memory? And if so, can it be learned?' *Scientific American*, 12 March. Available at www.scientificamerican.com/article/is-there-such-a-thing-as/#:~:text=The%20vast%20majority%20of%20the,likely%20to%20be%20an%20eidetiker, accessed on 22 June 2021.

2. *New Scientist* (no date) 'Photographic memory.' Available at www.newscientist.com/definition/photographic-memory, accessed on 22 June 2021.

3. McGowan, J. (no date) *Dyslexia and Working Memory*. Literacy Care and The Child Development Network. Available at www.literacycare.com.au/files/4313/9787/4403/Dyslexia_and_WM_-_Montessori_2014.pdf, accessed on 22 June 2021.

4. McGowan, J. (no date) *Dyslexia and Working Memory*. Literacy Care and The Child Development Network. Available at www.literacycare.com.au/files/4313/9787/4403/Dyslexia_and_WM_-_Montessori_2014.pdf, accessed on 22 June 2021.

5. Driver Youth Trust (2014) *The Fish in the Tree: Why We Are Failing Children with Dyslexia.* 28 March. London. Available at https://driveryouthtrust.com/fish-in-the-tree-report-and-drive-for-literacy, accessed on 25 February 2022.

6. Ibbetson, C. (2021) 'Can teachers and parents spot Dyslexia?' YouGov, 21 January. Available at https://yougov.co.uk/topics/education/articles-reports/2021/01/21/spot-dyslexia-symptoms-teachers-parents, accessed on 21 July 2021.

7. www.bdadyslexia.org.uk

8. https://dyslexiaida.org

Chapter 2

Colour, Creed and Circumstance

As a child, I know that I was incredibly fortunate to have been given the opportunity to take part in many activities. By the middle of Year 4 (age 8–9), I was having regular private tuition – four times a week, to be exact. I had piano lessons on a Monday, swimming lessons and debating classes midweek, and on a Saturday morning I would attend ballet, tap and gymnastic classes. I wanted to play tennis, but tennis classes were too expensive. That didn't stop my mum from making my dream a reality. She bought four rackets and a bucket of tennis balls. On most evenings she would take my brothers and me to our local park and we would play together, effectively teaching ourselves. A local tennis coach admired our determination and went out of his way to unofficially train us. So my routine as a child was full on and, at times, intense, but I thrived in that environment.

Keeping busy and trying new things excited me. My parents noticed that I had an ever-growing curious mind. My dad would always comment on my "wandering" mind. This upset me as a child, but as an adult, I see it as a backhanded compliment. I am very good at spinning many plates at once and doing an outstanding job on every project, task or job, despite doing more than one at the same time. I become bored very easily, and since childhood have struggled to focus on one thing for a long period. Sometimes my parents did not understand why I liked to keep myself preoccupied with so much to do. It was an expensive challenge, but my mum and dad did not shy away from it.

My parents worked tirelessly to provide as much opportunity for all four of their children but especially me, for a number of reasons. They wanted their children to break the glass ceiling. By that I mean my parents endured living a working-class life so that their children would not have to. Both of my parents are immigrants from Nigeria. Like many immigrants, they came to the UK in search of a better life. The reality of an immigrant's journey isn't often spoken of, but I watched both my mum and dad work for 18+ hours a day. I watched them create several side hustles and hold down various jobs in order to pay for the enriching activities and additional academic tuition that built my siblings and I into who we are today. I grew up knowing that my parents made several sacrifices so that I could shine. They always went the extra mile for me. I am and will always be especially grateful to them because I know that not all parents are able to do this, for many different reasons, including the multiple disadvantages they themselves may face.

For my parents, having me, a **female**, as their eldest child, made it especially important that I excelled in everything I did. In many cultures the eldest child holds a lot of responsibility, but in my parents' culture, the Igbo culture, the responsibility of the eldest child is even more significant. It's important that we dig a little deeper into what it means to be the eldest child for Igbo people. The eldest child is known as the "opara" – meaning the first **male** child born into any family. The "opara" leads the way for their siblings – everything stops and starts with him. It is believed that the first son is a symbol of hope for the family's continuity. If you haven't already realized, this is problematic for me because I was (and am) a female. As the "ada", the first-born female child as well as the eldest of my siblings, the cultural patriarchal hierarchy pitches everything against me. It could be argued that being born female makes everything I do insignificant. Being female means my capabilities ought to be limited.

It makes me so proud to say that my parents were keen to break this tradition. My dad was especially enthusiastic about raising the bar high for me – it wasn't about being male or female for him. My dad's belief is that all Igbo men should raise their eldest child, male or female, to be a good example that all their siblings would want to follow. Every child, and especially every first child, should be seen as a symbol of hope. His thinking was unusually modern, but important for my development. He empowered me to be a matriarch, a female "opara". This gave me an indescribable confidence. I may have struggled with reading, writing and spelling, but that was not going to stop me from achieving.

For both my mum and dad, it was important that my brothers saw me shine, because they believed that it would encourage them, too. From a sociological point of view, they did not want to raise boys who would grow into misogynistic men. They wanted my brothers to see me as a well-rounded, educated and courageous woman. My inability to spell, read and write properly wasn't something they wanted to focus on. This doesn't mean that they ignored my challenges – they fully acknowledged that I found certain tasks challenging, but that wasn't the focus of who I am.

For anyone who lives with a learning difference, feeling empowered and supported by those around you forges an opportunity to create your own success, no matter that you may have areas of difficulty. In a world where culturally and academically I should have been seen as a second-class citizen, my parents' decision to go against the grain led me to achieve unimaginable things. My hope is that in reading this book, you, too, will be inspired yourself to go out and try hard to achieve what you really want in life, despite the obstacles you will face.

Some academic papers state that there are more boys than girls with dyslexia. We have to question whether this is truly the case. Are there really more boys than there are girls with dyslexia, or are more boys being given access to the opportunity to explore neurodivergence? A group of academics in the US wrote a paper that concluded that more males are **diagnosed** with dyslexia than females.[1] There are several reasons for this, but my belief is that, generally, boys are raised to be more confident in finding solutions to problems. It is more socially and, in some cases, culturally, acceptable for a boy or man to probe, ask questions and investigate their difficulties.

Many girls and women who struggle with reading, writing and spelling will, like me, blame themselves for their inabilities rather than asking questions about their difficulties. My parents' decision to uplift me, mentally and culturally, is huge. Not only did they break out of a cultural norm that suppresses the confidence of women, as a child they made me know that I must sensibly question my academic challenges and not resort to blaming myself. In many cultures, girls and women are not encouraged to do this, so I share with you my parents' courageous parenting that saw them dare to be different in a bid to inspire you to do the same. If you're reading this and thinking about those times that you failed in your school spelling test, or perhaps a relative, your own child or a friend struggled to read something to you, ask questions and consider whether this needs further investigation. Discussing neurodivergence and, more specifically, dyslexia should not be considered a taboo in any culture.

You may wonder why I have taken the time to provide a detailed explanation of my heritage and ancestral culture. It's because in telling my story I want to unpack various factors that play a role in the discussion of dyslexia and neurodivergence more widely. I have also included it to encourage the development of cultural competence in society. You're probably wondering what I mean by "cultural competence". Throughout my time in formal education, this term was thrown around with the assumption being that everyone knew what it truly meant. Worryingly, little time is spent discussing its meaning and **why** it is important.

Put simply, cultural competence is the ability to understand and interact effectively with people from different cultures to your own. In order to be culturally competent, first, you must have a basic understanding of your own culture. You must be acutely self-aware (which is why I have taken the time to explore, understand and discuss my heritage). Second, you must have a willingness to learn about other people's cultural and historic practices. You need to have a desire to learn about the worldview of others. Finally, it's vital to have a positive attitude towards cultural difference – to respectfully accept differences in appearance and behaviour. I hope that by laying out the details of my own culture here, it will encourage you to think about details of your own culture, and the similarities and differences you have experienced.

Exploring my own socioeconomic background and culture has drawn out a few intersecting issues that

I want to bring your attention to. The first is that in certain cultures, the academic expectation for girls and women is lower than it is for boys and men. If you add the issue of neurodivergence to the topic of girls' education, you will find that girls end up with fewer opportunities to explore whether they have special educational needs or a learning difference. This inability to discover whether you are neurodivergent has detrimental effects. While these learning differences may not be realized when a young girl is in primary school, later in life, a lack of diagnosis will reduce her chances of employment, which makes it harder for girls and women to live independently. And in some cases, it may even encourage an unhealthy reliance on men. All of this creates gender inequity.

The second issue is social class. People from an under-served background are less likely to explore whether they have special educational needs. I was lucky to have parents who had the privilege of making sacrifices for me and for my siblings. You may find it odd that I say making a sacrifice is a privilege (in its own right). I say this because there are millions of families who simply cannot afford to make this sacrifice. Systems of oppression have made them so destitute that they must make do with what they have. My experience of working with under-served families in the UK has shown me that the systems that have been created with the intention of supporting families (benefits system, universal credit, income support) sometimes leave those families worse off. Additionally, many of these systems are founded on principles which do not reflect people's lived reality, for example, the assumption that everyone can read and write in English to fill in the forms or that everyone has a permanent address, which is often an eligibility criteria. The unfortunate reality is that this is not the case for too many people. There are people who cannot read for various reasons, one of which includes undiagnosed learning differences. It would be difficult for them to access any support on offer, these people are sadly left behind.

There are families who live in permanent survival mode, which means that extra academic tuition, sporting activities and other extra-curricular activities are not an option for them as they were for me. I use the term "under-served" rather than "disadvantaged" because "under-served" reflects the fact that there is a lack of resources, guidance and support. The poverty I am referring to is not a result of one section of society having more of an advantage than another; rather, my focus is on poverty caused by insufficient access to opportunity.

The third issue is race. My ethnicity and culture are at the centre of my experience. This is something that is often missed. We live in a world where the aim is "not to see" colour, creed or circumstance with the assumption that this will create equality. This is fundamentally wrong. The aim of equality means that communities are given the same resources and opportunities, although each community has a different starting point. Some communities will need more resources. The focus should be on creating equity. Equity recognizes that each community has different circumstances and cultures, so the resources and opportunities allocated and distributed differ in order to reach an equal outcome. Simply put, those who are starting on the back foot should be given a hand up rather than constantly being given access to a limited set of handouts they cannot always access.

The issues I have raised can be seen in our society. The under-served under-perform academically, and in some cases this is because they are not given the opportunity to discover their special educational needs or learning differences. There are certain cultures and traditions that do not pay attention to neurodivergence and, more worryingly, that may not acknowledge any academic challenges faced by girls and women in particular.

While the aim of this book is to spark a healthy conversation to stimulate the development of solutions to the problems listed above, I stress that it is important to be respectfully aware of cultural and traditional differences. The discussion of cultural competence and socioeconomic background is crucial if we want to increase access to opportunity for neurodivergent people.

I hope that whether you are a dyslexic young person, a policy-maker, a parent, a teacher or simply someone who is interested in neurodivergence and intersectionality, you will see from this part of my story that all these factors must be taken into account to ensure a fair society where everyone has the same opportunities to thrive.

Notes

1. Arnett, A.B., Pennington, B.F., Peterson, R.L., Willcutt, E.G., DeFries, J.C. and Olson, R.K. (2017) 'Explaining the sex difference in dyslexia.' *Journal of Child Psychology and Psychiatry* 58(6), 719–727. Available at www.ncbi.nlm.nih. gov/pmc/articles/PMC5438271, accessed on 25 July 2021.

Chapter 3

En Route to British Boarding School

Now on to the matter of investigation – where do we begin? I went through my entire primary schooling as an undiagnosed dyslexic. My parents and Year 3 schoolteacher had known that something was wrong, but they weren't sure about the exact challenge I was facing. It was good to know that I was no longer being blamed for my inability to read, write and spell properly. However, going through school knowing that something wasn't quite right, and not being able to identify why, wasn't great for my self-esteem. This is one of the reasons why my parents felt it was necessary to invest in extra-curricular activities and private academic tuition.

I'd like to give you a vivid picture of what a typical day looked like for eight-year-old me.

5:30am: My alarm goes off and my mum creeps into my bedroom and whispers words of encouragement to get up. We go for a jog in the local park, a stone's throw away from home.

6:15am: My mum watches me cross the road so I can return home and prepare for the day. She always stands at the park gate and watches me walk home with a smile on her face. I get showered and dressed for school. Then I sit at the dining table where my mum has left four test papers for me: English, Maths, Verbal Reasoning and Non-Verbal Reasoning. The aim would be to finish each paper in the allotted time.

I really struggled with this. Unknown to me at the time, I had a slower processing speed than my peers. A set of questions that I was instructed to have finished in 6 minutes would often take me 10. There were some mornings when I felt utterly hopeless. I was trying my hardest, but my efforts weren't showing up in my work. I did notice that whenever

I ignored the allotted timings, my scores were always higher, so I made a mental note that if I changed my thoughts on the concept of time, I would eventually be able to complete the tests in the time stated. It worked. I made myself believe that 6 minutes could feel like 10 minutes if I let go of the idea that I was running some sort of race.

Academia is often presented to children as if it's a sprint when in actual fact it's a marathon. I stopped using the timer that my mum had left out and decided to start by simply completing the task at hand. I would look at my watch when I started a test and look again when I finished it. As my confidence grew, the anxiety surrounding completing a task in a specific time frame disappeared. When I was ready, I reintroduced the timer and I was beginning to complete the tests in the allotted time. So, Monday–Friday, I completed four tests papers every morning before school.

8am: I have breakfast that my mum has prepared for me. It was always Rice Krispies topped with an indulgent amount of white sugar, covered in warm cow's milk. I enjoy the crackling sound as the Rice

Krispies expand with milk, the crunchy bowl of cereal quickly becoming an oddly satisfying, sweet and sloppy breakfast. While I eat I either watch BBC Breakfast News on TV or read a book, depending on my mood. The good thing about BBC Breakfast News is that they would often have either a Maths or English challenge going at the same time – my brothers and I would attempt to figure out the answer.

After this we walk to school with our mum, who somehow got herself ready at the same time as preparing four children and four lunches. Following school, I come home to a table full of snacks that I quickly gobble down and then I attend an extra-curricular activity or an academic tuition class. I am always in bed by 8:45pm – one of my mum's non-negotiables. If I am going to have a jam-packed day, I need to have enough sleep to enjoy it.

From reading the above, it's fair to say that I had a busy life for an eight-year-old and I absolutely loved each day. Being given the opportunity to do so many different things was great for my mind and diversified my thinking. While there is a common misconception that dyslexia only affects a person's ability to read, write and spell, the British Dyslexia Association has reported that it can also affect memory, organization, timekeeping, concentration, multitasking and communication. Unknown to my parents, my rather rigid routine and multifaceted schedule was an excellent way of helping me cope with my dyslexia.

You may not want to include quite as many elements into your own routine – make sure it works for you – but here are a few reasons why a schedule can help:

1. A daily routine helped me to stay organized. Dyslexic people can sometimes struggle with sticking to schedules and remembering appointments, and they have poor time management. My parents took that stress away from me at a young age by telling me what needed to happen and when. It may seem rather dictatorial, but the positive thing about it is that I have grown up knowing that routines work well for me and, as a young adult, I now ensure that my days are structured.

2. Having a week filled with different activities meant that I didn't get bored. I knew that I had a vast amount to get through, which forced me to stay focused on each task at hand. I didn't get frustrated about staying focused because I knew that I would soon be on to the next task and/or activity.

3. The vast array of extra-curricular activities helped build my self-esteem. I loved going to school but felt ashamed about my reading and writing abilities. My parents gave me the chance to do things outside of school that I became exceptionally good at. This helped me see that my reading and writing skills did not define me.

4. Getting enough sleep was a non-negotiable. Let's face it, dyslexic people have to work harder than others and often spend more time working than neurotypical people because the challenges we face can cause a delay in the delivery of our work. My 8:45pm bedtime meant that I was getting 8+ hours of sleep, so I didn't feel tired, and this reduced the likelihood of me then making mistakes in my academic work.

5. Having prompts helped jog my memory. Little things such as leaving out my breakfast and academic papers helped me remember to complete those tasks. It is often feared that prompting someone may encourage laziness. A common misconception is that prompting may stifle creativity or encourage forgetfulness. This isn't the case – prompting meant that my outstanding tasks were more likely to get done.

Aside from keeping me busy, my mum did have an agenda behind my busy routine. When I was in Year 4, she had a conversation with a friend about private secondary schooling. At this point, despite the challenges of being an undiagnosed dyslexic, I was at the top of my class in most subjects, and oddly, my best performance was in literacy. My mum's friend had explained that she was preparing her son to sit 11+ exams in order to attend either a grammar or private secondary school, and my mum asked her if it was something that I would be capable of achieving. My mum's friend encouraged her to put me through the 11+ exams and so she did.

My extra academic tuition served a potentially

life-changing purpose. The goal was to coach me in a way that would enable me to perform well enough to either be awarded a scholarship or bursary to attend a private school or to rank highly enough in my local 11+ exams, which would grant me a place at one of North London's most competitive grammar schools. I had three tutors: the first focused on national curriculum content, the second on mathematics and algebra and the third on the all-important verbal and non-verbal reasoning content that is needed for the 11+ exam. It was an intense process, and the very first time my academic progress was consistently being measured by test scores.

We are all different, and please do not think that I am writing this to encourage you to follow the same path as me. What worked for me, in lifting me and helping me achieve despite – and because of – my dyslexia may well be different for you. Some might argue that constant scrutiny of test scores puts too much pressure on a child. This may be true for some children, but I personally believe that this was one of the most character-building moments in my life. I was working at a disadvantage, and if I had been diagnosed, I would have been granted 25%

extra time. So I was always a step behind my peers. I had to create techniques to help me cope with exam pressure.

This is something that many primary schools do not prepare students for, because in the UK there are no public exams until children are aged 16 and 18 and do their GCSEs and A-Levels. Learning to cope with the rigour of academic exams aged 11 for the school application and 11+ tests ended up being invaluable to me. It set me up for secondary school. As a dyslexic I gained valuable experience in something that was always going to be harder for me than for non-dyslexic students. (Later I will tell you about how I was able to share the skills and tips I learnt with others through setting up my own tutoring business, Enrich Learning.) There were times when I failed the practice tests woefully, and several moments when I couldn't keep up with the tuition classes because there was an overload of information to process. There were moments when I simply wanted to give up, but I stayed determined. Wherever you are putting your energy, and wherever you are finding elements of difficulty in your life,

I hope my story will reassure you that you, too, can persevere through those difficulties and not give up.

In 2008, I visited a British boarding school in West Sussex called Christ's Hospital, one of the oldest boarding schools in England. It was built for children who were in need of access to a good education and social care. King Edward VI founded the school in 1552 following a passionate sermon delivered by the Bishop of London. Situated in London in the old buildings of Newgate Street, Christ's Hospital provided food, clothes, lodgings and learning for fatherless and poor men's children. Today, social mobility and philanthropy is still at the heart of the school's admissions process, with bursaries being awarded to 75% of its pupils.

From the very day I saw the school campus, my heart was set on attending the school as a secondary school pupil. All the students wore an odd Tudor-style uniform with heavy Dr Martens shoes. They marched in military style into the dining hall for lunch to a full live band. Some of the teachers wore university gowns that looked like superhero capes. It was all very surreal, as if we'd been teleported into the age of Hogwarts. It was different – and I was different – so I knew I would fit in. I was willing to do whatever it took, and my parents reassured me that if I won a place to attend the school, the teachers there would be able to provide me with greater support, meaning that my reading, writing and spelling would improve.

Why did my parents have so much faith in a school they'd never heard of prior to submitting my application? One reason was that they had heard about there being a difference between state and private education, especially for children with special educational needs. Whether this is always the case or not is open to question, and many state schools increasingly have excellent dyslexia and learning differences support, but this is what my parents believed at the time.

Having attended both private and state schools, I believe that my parents were right in believing there was a difference in the level of education, support and access to opportunity that a private school has to offer – although there are, of course, many exceptions. I want to explore this with you a little more, but before I do so, I want you to note one thing – the following discussion on private vs state schooling is not written to encourage elitism. As you've seen in my previous chapter about intersectional areas of inequity, lack of access to support and education can be a huge barrier to social mobility, wellbeing and more, for many people.

My personal entry to private school was based on merit, and while the majority of those who do attend private school pay their way into private education establishments, my experience is not at all reflective of that. I include this examination of private vs state education because I want to provoke a meaningful conversation where the stark differences between private and state schools in the UK are highlighted.

I believe that the inequity caused by the huge gap between the two schooling systems creates a caste-like class system that may seem impossible to break. I believe, like many others, that there are many changes to education that would narrow this gap, and that some groups, born of generations of wealth, have received unfair privileges, sometimes oppressing other groups. In the same breath, it's important that it's made clear that I am not anti-private school; I am pro-choice. What is needed is a better-equipped, well-funded state school system that enables children and young people, with or without special educational needs, the opportunity to create their own success. This is a matter for educational policy, which, in turn, requires a greater understanding of the underlying issues around gender, class and race, an understanding this book is intended to further.

In 2019, the British Dyslexia Association said the diagnosis and support for children with dyslexia was the worst it had been since the government started funding for it in the 1980s. By law, publicly funded schools and local authorities must make an effort to identify and assess children with suspected dyslexia; however, limited access to assessment has made it near impossible for some children to get the diagnosis they deserve and are legally entitled to.

An estimated 870,000 children are reported to have dyslexia, but fewer than 150,000 of them have been diagnosed, according to Department of Education figures as reported by BBC News.[1] To put that into context for you, **only 17% of suspected dyslexic children have been formally diagnosed.** Sharon Hodgson MP, quoted by BBC News, noted that the children who go undiagnosed are from under-served communities and schools; in her words, "there is a clear poverty divide".[2] State schools simply do not have enough money to afford the assessments or support for those who are actually fortunate enough to receive a formal assessment and diagnosis.

My experience echoes Sharon Hodgson's message. I am from an under-served community, with very little access to funding for special educational needs assessment. For my parents, a private school funded by a scholarship or bursary was their only hope of me being given the support and opportunity necessary for me to maximize my potential. Throughout my state primary school education, despite my teachers knowing I was facing a challenge that indicated that I had special educational needs, I was never offered the opportunity to be assessed because they did not have the funding for it. The best they could do was to ask parents to volunteer their time to help children like me practise my reading skills at a slower pace than my peers.

Diagnostic assessments are inaccessible for many families (many of whom may not even realize for cultural or other reasons that dyslexia could be an issue!) because they are expensive. I want to dig a little deeper into the cost of an assessment as this will help you have a greater understanding of the inaccessibility I am referring to.

The average cost of a dyslexia assessment is £485 (US$654) with a specialist teacher and £600 (US$810) with an educational psychologist.[3] The average family income in the UK currently stands at £2,491 (US$3,273) a month.[4] With a limited number of assessments available in schools, the responsibility to get a proper assessment often falls on the shoulders of parents. It's time we begin to consider how many households can afford to spare an extra £485 or £600 in order to pay for an assessment. The truth is, not many.

Alarmingly, the corporate assessment service assessments funded by schools, local authorities, universities, organizations and employers – is more expensive. Corporate assessments cost £540 (US$729) with a specialist teacher and £720 (US$972) with an educational psychologist.[5]

With funding cuts on the rise, school leaders and educators are being forced to make difficult decisions, such as limiting the number of life-changing assessments available to their pupils.

In recent years, there has been an endeavour to, at the very least, give someone the opportunity to explore whether they have dyslexia through a dyslexia screening test. These screening tests are designed to give people an indication of potential dyslexic difficulties, and are easier to access than the expensive full diagnostic assessments. They can be accessed online and are provided by a wide range of facilitators at different price points. In my view, they are an attempt to bridge the gap between not having a diagnostic assessment and having an awareness, albeit sometimes vague, of dyslexic difficulties. While they can be a useful indicator that a diagnostic assessment might be helpful, they don't replace one, as they would not lead to students being able to access reasonable adjustments in exams, for example.

There are many different types of screening tests. Some are delivered by a computer while others are carried out by a schoolteacher or special educational needs coordinator (SENCo). They vary in the amount of information they can give a candidate. Some give an estimate as to whether a child or adult is likely to have dyslexic difficulties. A small number of tests give candidates a profile of strengths and weaknesses that can help inform teachers and parents on the best teaching strategy for the potentially dyslexic person. Screening tests are more accessible due to the low, and in some cases, no cost. However, they **do not** provide a formal diagnosis. Meaningful adjustments for formal exams cannot be made without a formal diagnosis.

It is, however, unreasonable to say that screening tests serve no purpose. In some ways they can help parents and schools save a lot of money. If someone does a screening test and it is found that they do not have any dyslexic difficulties, a pricey diagnostic assessment with a specialist teacher or educational psychologist would not then be needed. On the flip side, if someone completes a screening test that confirms the suspicions of dyslexia and they cannot afford a diagnostic assessment, they are then stuck between a rock and a hard place. By this

I mean that they are forced to go about their daily lives knowing that they have a learning difference, but with no way of accessing formal support. Sometimes schoolteachers use the results from a screening test to provide additional support for children with learning differences, and this is great. However, this is out of goodwill as opposed to the professional support that is required to maximize a child's potential.

Difficulties in accessing and affording these all-important diagnostic assessments further leads to unequal outcomes, not only in schools, but also in the working world. A lack of assessment when someone is a child means that they go into the workforce ill equipped, having not been taught the skills they need to survive and thrive in a neurotypical world. It also lowers their chances of gaining entry to higher education institutions. For all these reasons, my parents encouraged me to work hard and to try to win a scholarship or bursary-funded place at a private school where they knew the life-changing opportunity to be supported and taught by specialists would be offered to me.

When my mother opened the large white envelope on Saturday 14 February 2009, the course of my destiny was set. I had won a place to attend Christ's Hospital. With the right support anyone can change the course of their destiny. In my case it was the 11+ and private schooling. It does not have to be the same for you. Having a conversation with a teacher, university lecturer or a friend who is familiar with your problems may help you gain a greater understanding of the challenges you are facing, and maybe get higher grades, or have the support to develop the self-understanding to pick the right exam subjects for you that you can really enjoy and become passionate about.

On reflection, I wish my parents and I had known about the various organizations that have been set up to provide additional support to those with dyslexia or who suspect they have dyslexia. In my adult life, I have since used the free online resources provided by the British Dyslexia Association, and they have helped me immensely.

Notes

1. BBC News (2019) 'Schools "failing to diagnose at least 80% of dyslexic pupils".' 25 October. Available at www.bbc.co.uk/news/uk-england-50095218, accessed on 25 July 2021.

2. BBC News (2019) 'Schools "failing to diagnose at least 80% of dyslexic pupils".' 25 October. Available at www.bbc.co.uk/news/uk-england-50095218, accessed on 25 July 2021.

3. British Dyslexia Association (no date) 'Diagnostic assessments.' Available at www.bdadyslexia.org.uk/services/assessments/diagnostic-assessments/overview#:~:text=The%20cost%20of%20an%20assessment,(%C2%A3600%20%2B%20VAT), accessed on 9 August 2021.

4. ONS (2020) 'Average household income, UK: financial year 2020.' Available at www.ons.gov.uk/peoplepopulationandcommunity/personalandhouseholdfinances/incomeandwealth/bulletins/householddisposableincomeandinequality/financialyear2020, accessed on 29 March 2022.

5. British Dyslexia Association (no date) 'Diagnostic assessments.' Available at www.bdadyslexia.org.uk/services/assessments/diagnostic-assessments/overview, accessed on 9 August 2021.

Chapter 4

Secondary Education...
Struggles and Solutions

Wednesday 9 September 2009 was my first day at
Christ's Hospital. It is still crystal clear in my mind
(thanks to the gift of my photographic memory).
My parents and I walked up four flights of rustic
stairs – no carpet, just varnished wood – and were
welcomed into what would be my first bedroom
at the school. I was sharing with two other girls
who were also new to the school. Mum and Dad
unpacked my suitcase while I gathered my bearings.
As they made up my bed, I was taken to collect my
uniform from Matron's Office.

The school uniform at Christ's Hospital is unique, and took some getting used to! I was given a shirt, bands (similar to the clerical bands that barristers wear), bright mustard-yellow socks, a skirt and a Tudor-style ladies' jacket. This was now my everyday attire. I was shown the process of putting it on, and to this day the order in which you put the uniform on is still with me, although it took me an age to get dressed every morning for a while – double the time of my peers. I found it difficult to master the process and order in which the uniform was to be worn. For children with learning differences, school uniform can be an issue because wearing it correctly requires organizational skills that some children don't have, or they may have motor coordination issues. I found it helpful to give myself more time to get dressed, and to lay things out the night before, perhaps in the order of wearing them!

Once I was dressed in my new uniform, I headed downstairs, eager to say goodbye to my parents so that I could begin my new life at this eclectic school. My dad gleamed with pride as he took photographs to commemorate this very special day, I distinctly remember my mum looking very deeply into my eyes and asking me if I would be okay. As an adult, I can now see that she was contemplating whether she had made the right decision to send me to a school 71 miles away from home. I naively reassured her, giving her a kiss on the cheek, and rushed away into the "day room" (the communal living space) to join another new Year 7 (age 11–12) child, who has now become a lifetime best friend.

The first couple of weeks were an adventure. There was always so much to do, and my timetable was filled with activity, from the moment I woke up to the moment I went to bed. I think this was done intentionally to help us settle in and avoid homesickness. But I struggled to keep up. My dyslexia means that it takes me a little longer to complete tasks, which isn't at all helpful when you're living in an environment where everything is timed to the second.

The day started with 40 bells at 7:15am. There was absolutely no chance of oversleeping because those bells rang loudly. Somehow we were expected to squeeze in a shower and get to breakfast by 7:30am. I quickly realized that I couldn't get showered and dressed in 15 minutes so, to the dismay of my roommates, I started waking up at 6:30am so that I could get ready without feeling rushed. By 8:00am we needed to be back in the boarding house where we would clean our teeth and, if scheduled, head downstairs to Matron's Office for a dress inspection.

The house roll call was at 8:10am where a senior pupil would read out the house register – sometimes you could still hear the sleep in their voices. By 8:20am we were out of the door, and in my case, power walking to lessons with a school bag the size of a torso on my back. We had 35-minute lessons from 8:30am to 11:05am, and a 20-minute break, where we all gobbled down toast and Jammie Dodgers biscuits. We then had two more 35-minute lessons before a 35-minute lunch break that included the march into lunch with the full marching band I mentioned earlier. The afternoon was packed with activities that ranged from sports to crafts.

I liked the fact that our lessons were short. As I've mentioned, I have something of a wandering mind, and so the 35-minute lessons were the perfect amount of time for me to be able to hyper-focus. However, I almost never finished the classwork or note-taking, if there was any. The words on the board always moved around, playing tricks on me. If the teacher wrote in green pen on a whiteboard, I couldn't read it at all.

At the end of the lesson, we would have to pack up our books and head to the next class. I was **always** last. I liked to pack my bag in a specific order so that I wouldn't mix up resources or subject-specific books. My pencils always had to be facing the same way in my pencil case – this took an age to arrange – and if I had a folder with me, everything was tabulated, or colour-coded. If I skipped out on any of the above "rituals", I would be miserable for the rest of the day. My little self-satisfying habit would creep into my lesson time, but I couldn't let it go. I started prepping for the end of the lesson 10 minutes before the actual end time, which meant that I was losing valuable learning time. And I would practise my "ritual" so quietly that most teachers hardly noticed, until my academic performance started to slip.

We were given 5 minutes to get from one class to another, and while for many pupils in more conventional schools that is plenty of time, in my case, it was not. My school campus covers 1,200 acres. I had classes that took me from the east end of the school to the west end – whoever created our timetables clearly didn't consider the logistics of travelling a mile in five minutes. In addition to that, all pupils wear heavy Dr Martens shoes – creating the perfect storm for any child to be late. A number of my teachers were either ex-military or had a love for the cadet force, so being on time for a lesson was especially important to them. For the first three weeks I ran, or, at the very least, speed-walked everywhere. My puberty "puppy fat" dropped off quickly.

I found navigating around the school really hard too. We were given mentors by the teachers – students in the year above us assigned to support us. Our mentor was responsible for us on arrival and had three weeks to show us the ropes. My mentor was so kind to me and noticed that I was utterly rubbish at reading maps. She took the time to drop me off at every lesson, even when the other mentors had stopped delivering that service for their own year sevens.

One day, my mentor must've forgotten to collect me from a class and I had another lesson to get to. As usual, I was last to leave because I was practising my bag-packing ritual. My peers had gone ahead of me to the science class – I had absolutely no idea where it was, as it was our first science lesson. I looked at the map, took a deep breath, and hoped for the best. I made my way to the Old Science School, walked into the first class I saw and took a seat at the back. It was dark because the class was watching a video clip.

Everyone in the classroom was considerably bigger than the peers I had left in my previous class. It was a physics lesson and the video clip was on a topic about forces that I still could not explain to you today. A pupil looked back and said loudly, "Has anyone else noticed that there is a year seven in the room?" The class teacher immediately reprimanded the boy for singling me out and making me feel bad. I blushed from head to toe, I felt so awful. The entire class burst out laughing at me and tears came to the forefront of my eyes. I kept telling myself that no matter what, I could not let one of those tears drop, and I didn't. I felt embarrassed because I had spent 20 minutes in a Year 13 (age 17–18) physics lesson, and had not realized. I was now very late to my class, I had no idea where my lesson was being held, and I was the joke of the day for the senior pupils.

The class teacher pitied me. She set class work for the Year 13 students, asked for my timetable and escorted me to my science lesson. I remember asking her if I would be getting into trouble for going to my next class 20 minutes late. She gave me a reassuring smile and promised to have a word with my teacher. I finally arrived at my science class, which was taking place exactly above the Year 13 physics lesson – my map reading skills were not as inaccurate as I thought. I had simply forgotten to consider the staircase in the building. I settled into my lesson rather quickly. Thankfully it was a double period and my peers were really nice to me about what had happened. My feelings of embarrassment quickly became a distant memory.

Now that we have a clear understanding of how

dyslexia can impact aspects of your life outside of academia, **I want to illustrate, using my own experience, the numerous challenges** that many dyslexics face on a daily basis, and hopefully help others who may have had similar problems on starting secondary school! Let's begin with time management.

When I was at secondary school, I struggled to complete tasks in the times allocated, and just about made it to class on time. Everyone else was able to keep up with the demanding school routine, but I was like a fish out of water. On reflection, I now know it's because dyslexia affects the way information is processed, stored and retrieved. Dyslexic people tend to have a slower processing speed. Not only does this make it difficult to estimate passages of time; it also forces you to think in a linear manner because time is a linear concept. I do not enjoy linear thinking – I never have. I'm sure many dyslexic people can relate to feeling "abnormal" because "normal" things, like getting to class on time, or packing up your school bag, are arduous tasks for us. We have to actively shift our mindsets to think in a neurotypical way when we are, in fact, neurodivergent.

In my case, I was scrambling between learning how to process, store and retrieve my school timetable and the directions to class while also trying to settle into a totally new environment. I had come from inner-city London to rural West Sussex. I experienced something of a culture shock when I realized that red buses and the tube line cannot be found throughout the UK – for your information, the buses in Horsham are multiple shades of blue. I had gone from asking "When is dinner time?" to "When is teatime?" – this may seem insignificant, but there were so many changes to my language pattern; at 11 years old, it's a lot to keep up with. At any secondary school you may experience big changes to things you have become used to at primary school.

The transition from primary to secondary school is huge. Children can find it both overwhelming and challenging. I don't think a child can ever be fully prepared for this change, but it can be made easier through conversations about what the child might expect. Regardless of the type of secondary school a child attends, there are common elements of secondary school that are likely to be unfamiliar to most children, which a child can be notified of prior to them starting. It would have been helpful for me to know that my secondary school timetable would have more than 12 subjects on it. When I saw my timetable for the first time I was mortified, and wondered how I would be able to cope with the demands of secondary school study. This led me to spend the majority of my first couple of weeks at secondary school in panic mode. Honest conversations between child and parent or teacher are also good for dispelling any myths of the "horrors" of secondary school. If you're a parent, create space for your child to be inquisitive and to ask questions.

Within the first three weeks of being at secondary school, I crammed my timetable to save me the time and effort required to lug it around in my torso-sized school bag. I then used muscle memory to get me to and from class. I couldn't bear the thought of trying to read the school map. To this day, I do not understand how anyone thought an 11-year-old would be able to navigate an A4 sheet of paper with font size 9 labels and arrows. My peers were able to use the map with ease; I could not. I felt ashamed, but tried my best to hide it. I clung on to other students and made an effort to ensure that I didn't go anywhere by myself. I had a particularly special bond with my roommate-turned-lifetime-best friend. I think she subconsciously noticed I was having a tough time and showed me that there is humour in everything. Friendships are really important in your pubescent years (more about this later).

While the short and sharp lessons were great for keeping me focused, they were a complete nightmare when I struggled in a subject. I have always been heavily reliant on my memory, especially because my map reading skills and sense of direction are rather poor. I distinctly remember sitting in my maths classes thinking "This is all a blur to me". By the time I understood how to solve an equation, the lesson had come to an end.

In summary, the combination of assimilating into a new culture while using my memory to do absolutely everything exhausted me. I didn't want to look like I wasn't coping. After all, this was what I wanted. To write an email expressing my challenges to my mum, who already sensed that I might find it hard to fit in, would be cruel. I knew my mum was worried and I didn't want her to pull me out of the school. Instead, I fell back into masking my dyslexia, just as I did in primary school. I spent hours cramming things.

I have one distinct memory where I spent hours cramming my first French vocabulary list. Rather than admitting that I didn't know how to process the new information, I stared blankly at the sheet of paper for hours. I remembered the words, thanks to my photographic memory, but I hadn't a clue what any of them meant. In the short term I appeared to be doing well; in the long term it became evident that I was struggling. This kind of masking or camouflaging can be a common experience for dyslexics and can result in huge psychological strain for us.

Before I carry on with detailing my first-year secondary school experience. I want to give you some tips on how to settle into a new environment.

Dyslexic people (and neurodivergent people generally) can find it hard to adjust to change. Here are a few things I could have done to make my life easier at the time:

1. "Fail to plan...plan to fail." This is a rather famous saying, and there aren't enough words to express its relevance for dyslexic people. Change can cause additional stress, which can worsen the symptoms of dyslexia that include: poor spelling, confusing the order of letters in words, putting letters and figures the wrong way round (such as writing 9 instead of 6 or b instead of d), slow writing speed, poor handwriting, visual disturbances when reading (such as blurred words or words that move around the page), difficulty carrying out a sequence of directions and poor phonics skills. Here are some specific planning tips...

    a) If you're being based in a new environment (e.g., starting a new school), take a guided tour of the environment **before** the new term/season starts. This will enable you to use your muscle memory more effectively.

b) Make Google Maps or Citymapper your friend. Use GPS tracking-style mapping apps to help you get from a to b. These maps are great because they give you a visual aid as well as audio instructions and a large icon that follows you as you make your way to your destination. If you take a wrong turn, it will correct you. This can help keep your stress levels low.

c) Pack your bag the night before (this tip is not limited to school students – people of all ages can do this to get a head start). This will stop you from over-packing and having a torso-sized backpack, like me.

d) In class or meetings, ignore the urge to unpack the entire contents of your bag unnecessarily. Take out what you need, when you need it...then put it straight back into your bag. This will prevent the development of bag-packing rituals, which will take up valuable time.

2. Reach out for help! It is better to let someone

know when you're struggling than to suffer in silence. In my case, I could have reached out to my houseparent – the member of staff assigned to look after me – or my form tutor. For you, that support may come from a parent or line manager. Either way, speak up when you're having a hard time.

3. Don't try to do everything at once. When I started secondary school, I was so excited to be there that I did **everything**. I played two instruments, played sport and took part in house activities. I became over-stimulated, overwhelmed and exhausted. I was constantly playing catch-up. A better approach would have been to phase things in slowly. By doing so I would have known just how far I could push myself before burnout.

The great difference between this school and my primary school is that the teachers did not fall into the trap of believing I was okay. Instead, they spent the first couple of weeks observing me. They watched me running around the school as I tried to keep up, they turned a blind eye to my bag-packing ritual, and they made a note of my rapidly declining academic grades – which were as a result of me never finishing any classwork, but always completing homework because I created more time for myself by waking up early.

After one evening roll call, my houseparent asked me to stay behind. She took me to her office and on the short walk to the office door, I ran through all the things I thought I may have forgotten. I was sure I hadn't been late to any classes – two weeks of running/speed-walking everywhere gets you fit quickly. I had never been a disobedient child (fun fact: I went through all my schooling without ever receiving a detention – I was a proud goodie two-shoes). I had handed in all my prep (homework) on time, although I'll admit I never finished It in the allocated prep time because, unknown to me at the time, my processing speed did not allow me to. I would wake up at the crack of dawn (sorry, roommates) and complete any outstanding tasks then. In actual fact, my prep was always immaculate. I took pride in my work, especially its appearance. I would obsess over the neatness of it, often starting the work from scratch if I had made a mistake. I was constantly trying to make my work perfect (I used perfectionism to mask my dyslexia). With all this in mind, what could my houseparent possibly want to speak to me about?

She sat me down and asked me how I thought things were going. I said I thought things were going well. I am a terrible liar and should have just been open and honest about the fact that I was exhausted by constantly living as though I were on the back foot. My houseparent had a habit of referring to all the girls as "chickens". This may seem odd to you, but I thought it was really sweet. She asked me again, this time including the term of endearment, "Chicken, how are things going?" I immediately felt more comfortable and explained that I was struggling, but, like most, if not all 11-year-old dyslexics, I did not understand why. After all, I had passed the entrance exam just like everybody else, so I was just as clever. Why couldn't I keep up and why was I, very evidently, working so much harder than my peers? It all seemed grossly unfair.

That evening I was excused from evening prep time and instead, was sent to the Teaching and Learning Department to see the members of staff

there. It was one of the most interesting evenings
I ever had in my seven years at the school. It was
also the first time I went to a location in the school
without getting lost in the process of getting there
– my muscle memory was beginning to work. The
staff members were incredibly kind. I first met
some of the teachers and was later introduced to
Mrs G. They calmly explained that there might be
a reason why I was finding it hard to cope. Like any
pubescent child, I initially challenged the idea that
I was struggling, but they came back at me with
explicit examples that ranged from the fact that
they had seen me always moving with haste, and
that my teachers had collectively noticed the several
blank pages of classwork. They also gave me the
really nice biscuits (at boarding school, Party Rings
were saved for special occasions). The meeting
ended with an invitation to attend an assessment
later that week. They reassured me that this was
not a test, meaning that there was no need to
practise and call on my usual perfectionism. It was
impossible to prepare or revise for it – all I needed to
do was show up and be myself.

I was quite excited for the assessment, and I rushed

back to my boarding house to tell my houseparent I had a test later on in the week. She seemed pleased. I guess she knew it was a diagnostic assessment. I, on the other hand, was none the wiser. I didn't tell her or any of the girls in my house about the Party Rings. Those biscuits were considered gold.

The assessment was an unusual experience. There was no English or maths. Instead I had to do rather strange activities, like write out the same sentence multiple times under time conditions. I was asked to repeat number sequences backwards, with each sequence increasing by one digit each time. My spelling was assessed too. I have intentionally erased that part of the assessment from my memory because I was so bad at it. My paper was collected and within a matter of days I was called into one of the teacher's offices and was told that I had a "learning difficulty" called "dyslexia". I was gutted.

I think the phrase that threw me is "learning difficulty". Throughout my childhood, having a "learning difficulty" was seen as a bad thing. This was for a couple of reasons, the first being that I had only ever seen learning differences as a problem that prevented me from being clever. While my primary school teachers and parents knew and accepted that I had academic challenges, there was no label for it. Strangely, they were comfortable with this purgatory status. For them, a lack of diagnosis meant that my academic troubles were temporary, something they could fix through the right support and encouraging me to work hard. The second reason is that, culturally, any discussion about learning differences is considered a taboo, as I have already mentioned earlier in this book. Learning differences are not spoken about in ethnic communities, and when conversation about them starts, it is quickly dismissed.

You may have noticed that until this point I have referred to "learning difficulties" as "learning differences". I have done this intentionally. I think it's important that we re-frame how neurodivergence is spoken about. Being dyslexic shouldn't be seen as a difficulty. I know that if I had been told that I had a "difference" as opposed to a "difficulty" my self-esteem would have been much higher than it was. No one wants to be told that they're living with a "difficult" condition.

I sat there with dread and fear. In my mind I told myself that I would be unable to develop intelligence. I went as far as telling myself that perhaps I wouldn't make it past my first year at the school. Additionally, I considered myself to be a walking taboo in my community because I had this learning difficulty called "dyslexia". This genuinely was my thought process, and I didn't have the words to explain this; I was, after all, a child. A series of questions ran through my mind with the most important one being "How on earth do I explain this to my Nigerian parents?" The pressure to tell my parents was eased by the fact that I did not have a phone and I communicated with them via email...this was before the days where children had smartphones. I decided instantly that this would be an in-person conversation that I had with my parents when I had a better understanding of my situation.

The teachers must have sensed my unease and disappointment. They pulled out a folder, and while they unpacked its contents, they spoke about the gifts of being neurodivergent. They reassured me that I wasn't "dumb", and suggested that I may be more intelligent than my peers if we took the time to figure out my "learning style" (more on this later). The contents of the folder were laid out before me in a neat line. There were three photographs of notable dyslexic people – Richard Branson, Jamie Oliver and Albert Einstein. The teachers took time to describe their incredible careers, and essentially told me that I should be chuffed because my brain was similar to theirs. Was it really, though?

These were loaded examples for a black, working-class, young girl. Apart from being dyslexic, what did I have in common with these men? These examples made me feel like an "other" in my own community, and I convinced myself that this was why learning differences were considered taboo in my community. It seemed that learning differences were for white men, and for white men only. Of course, this is absolutely not the case. Learning differences do not attach themselves to a specific colour, creed or circumstance; anyone from any background can have a learning difference, but we need to see this to believe it.

Unfortunately, the examples I was shown reflected

one colour, one gender, and, to a certain degree, one creed as well, as people with circumstances that were totally out of touch from my own. I mean, Albert Einstein had been dead for 54 years at the time, when he was being used as an example of a successful dyslexic. It's important to note that the teachers and the school were not in any way to blame for using these examples. Many schools and websites do the same thing. They were doing their very best to support me with the resources that were available at the time.

I ran a Google search on black people with dyslexia, and the only person who showed up was Whoopi Goldberg. To make matters worse, Google swapped "dyslexia" with "dyscalculia". It is likely that if any dyslexic black child tries to search the internet seeking out an example of a dyslexic who is similar to them, they would be largely unsuccessful in their quest. The big question now is how do we change this? After all, this book is about bringing you solutions, and I haven't written it to rehash problems. So here are my suggestions:

1. Organizations that have centred themselves

around dyslexia and neurodiversity more widely need to build a portfolio of diverse ambassadors. For too long the dyslexic community has been shown the same faces – and these faces tend to be white, male and middle-aged. It's time for a change.

2. Educational institutions need to make greater efforts in showing their students that learning differences don't look a specific way. Assemblies and personal tutor/form tutor sessions are great ways of regularly communicating the message that not only is it okay to have a learning difference, but it's also something to celebrate as well as be proud of.

3. Mainstream media, literature and entertainment ought to create space on their platforms for neurodivergent people. Although in recent years it is apparent that more thought than ever before has gone into giving neurodivergent people airtime, I believe it is time to push the boundaries further. It's not enough to have airtime for 1 out of 52 weeks to showcase the amazing gifts of neurodivergence. It needs to become part of

regular scheduling in order to dismantle the myth that neurodivergence and learning differences are "abnormal".

4. Last, and most importantly, as individuals we must learn to honour difference. We can do this by simply accepting that everyone is different. A lot of effort goes into making human beings similar from an early age. For example, in most schools children are made to wear the same uniform and they're given the same exams, despite their differences in cognitive ability. It is good and important for society to have elements of homogeneity, but we must remember that we all start from different places. This is why I advocate for equity rather than equality. Equity recognizes difference and creates the space to celebrate it.

My dyslexia diagnosis made me aware of just how different I am in comparison to my peers. My difference empowered me to start a business at the tender age of 12. I started the business because I had a vision and a dream. I was not going to allow dyslexia to stop me. If you're reading this and, like me, you're dyslexic or have something that makes you different from your peers, don't let your difference stop you.

I realize that I have dropped a bit of a bombshell, with my entrepreneurial journey starting so young. It's only fair that I now dive into how it all began in the hope that it will inspire you to get your vision and dreams started, whenever you're ready.

Chapter 5

Building Enrich Learning

My life as a businesswoman started on my return home from my first year of boarding school. Despite the challenges of settling into a new environment and adjusting to life as a diagnosed dyslexic, I was enthused about what the future held for me. My first year at Christ's Hospital had opened my mind, and in many ways gave me this unending feeling of empowerment. I can't quite find the words to explain how being in that environment inspired me, but what I can say is that being out of my comfort zone, in a somewhat foreign setting and coping with it well, made me truly believe that I could do anything I put my mind to. I had proved to myself that I could be both fearless and independent. I wanted to show my family what I had learnt in my first year away from home in a unique manner, and I felt the best way to do this would be in the form of my own project that would not only keep me entertained, but also make me some pocket money too.

Within the first two weeks of my summer holiday, I asked my mum if I could assist some children with their school homework for a small fee. I was already shadowing her and her colleagues at the pre-school where she is a keyworker and, in my time there, I found that I connected with the children. I especially enjoyed assisting the toddlers with their activities, but, admittedly, I felt I needed something that would stimulate my mind. I wanted something that would challenge me.

My mum didn't need much convincing, and, after a few calls, she found my first student. I started supporting this child with their homework for a fee of £5 for an hour's session. I didn't like Mathematics very much, so I only provided homework support in their English studies. Even at 12 years old I knew my strengths and I worked with them. I knew that there was no point in pushing myself to do something I wasn't great at, and where I was delivering a **paid** service, it was important to me that I was offering good value for money and enjoyed what I was doing. Even with being dyslexic, English was undoubtedly my strongest subject. Supporting this student with their homework confirmed my abilities and gave me buckets of confidence. Neurodivergent or not, it's important that you have a strong sense of what you're good at. Know your craft, and then work on it. Be limitless in your approach, and don't fear failure.

The tuition sessions with my first student were thoroughly enjoyable. To begin with, the student would bring their school homework and we would complete it together. We soon completed the homework more quickly and I started to plan additional work to do in the sessions. I knew what my barriers to entry in terms of teaching were. I would practise the spelling tests the night before. You can find lots of dyslexia-friendly techniques for spellings online – discover what works best for you or the person you are supporting. I began to take a real interest in the student's development and set targets for them in order to help them not only succeed, but to be the very best in their class.

My efforts paid off. The student's parents reported significant positive changes in their school grades and school reports. Their mother expressed an interest in the 11+ exams, but noted that she couldn't afford the price of what 11+ tutors were demanding at the time. I immediately saw a gap in the market. At that point in time, I didn't see myself as a 12-year-old who was providing homework support in order to make a little pocket money so that I could go to the cinema; I saw myself as a businesswoman with a sense of purpose.

Part of the reason why I went to a boarding school 71 miles away from home was because the access to opportunity for all children with learning differences in Edmonton was (and sadly still is) poor. The local comprehensive secondary schools were under-performing, and my parents had seen too many young people with masses of potential not have the chance to maximize their greatness because the educational provision for them was inadequate.

I must emphasize that I'm not anti-comprehensive schooling; in my case, my parents felt that none of the local comprehensive schools at the time were equipped to provide me, as a dyslexic, with the education that my parents believed I deserved. As I have explained, they hadn't sought a formal dyslexia diagnosis for me for a variety of reasons, and that meant I would not have gained the support someone on the special educational needs register might have. Although there are comprehensive schools that are providing outstanding education for their pupils, including those with learning differences, I didn't live in an area where we believed that was available to me. What school you go to, and what support you get there, can make a huge difference to your confidence, learning and self-esteem if you're neurodivergent. As awareness grows, and we make the sorts of changes listed above, this should, I hope, improve.

In my first year away from Edmonton I had been exposed to opportunities that I previously thought would never have been made available to me. Most importantly, I was receiving a first-class education that made me believe that I could do anything that

I wanted to do. I then felt an incomprehensible
sense of duty to impart what I had learnt, and had
seen not only the student I had in front of me, but
many children and young people I could also reach.
I didn't want to be the only person from Edmonton
to have had access to a superb education. This is
not to say that the schools in the area were not
trying, but they were under-served, under-funded
and under-staffed.

The chances my student had of maintaining
their new levels of success were slim. I agreed to
take them on for 11+ preparation, which would
potentially gain them entry into a selective school.
While my main intention was to help, I won't shy
away from the fact that I also saw an opportunity
to make some pocket money. There was a gap in
the market in the sense that people wanted 11+
tuition but had little to no access to it, because of
cost. At the time, the most affordable tuition was
being delivered at £25 (US$34) per hour. I dropped
the price to £7 (US$9.45) an hour. The student's
mother very happily accepted my fee, and the hard
work began. I revisited all my 11+ books, taking extra
care to make note of the techniques I had used to

succeed. I reflected on what I had done that had enabled me to pass the exams, and started to teach my student my unique methods. While I used my own experience to help others taking the 11+, the methods I developed, I later realized, applied much more widely, to exam skills more generally.

After two weeks I asked my mum if she could find more students for me. I had come to understand that if I taught more than one student at a time, not only could I make more money, but I could also increase my value proposition – I could make access to tuition more affordable and so help a larger number of students. My mum agreed, and sourced more students through her network. She told a friend, who told a friend, who told a friend you get the picture. I soon had four students sitting around our dining room table taking 11+ tuition from me. I increased my prices to £10 (US$13.49), and also increased the session time to 90 minutes as I came to recognize that one hour simply wasn't enough time if I was going to teach thoroughly. This meant that my hourly rate was £6.67 (US$8.99)! This was (and in many cases still is) unheard of.

I'm competitive by nature, and in this case it was immensely helpful because it meant I really cared about the outcome of these tuition sessions. I wanted all the students I taught to pass their 11+ exams and to have the opportunity to choose which secondary school they would attend as opposed to accepting whatever the local authority assigned to them. Choice has always been important to me because it is a symbol of freedom. My tutoring services, if done well, would enable my students and their parents the freedom to choose what their future looked like. While this did put me under pressure, I found it encouraging, because to me, it meant I was making a difference if I got things right...and I did.

My first set of students ended up passing their 11+ exams as well as coming top in the SATs exams (end of primary school tests at age 11). One of them was awarded a place at an international school in East Africa. The key thing was that they had received a boost to their education that was affordable to their families, at the critical time of choosing a secondary school. I am aware that this is still not something that is available to many people. Using education as a tool, I helped my students and their parents be the authors of their own stories in the sense that they could write their own destiny. What other dyslexic kids and young people can take from this is that they, too, can change their own stories, whatever obstacles they face. This might be improving their SATs results and therefore their GCSE predictions, if that's what's important to them, by engaging with the many educational tools that are available online now. Or it could be applying themselves intensively to some other activity they love, like music or football. And if you're a bit older, or you've got really good at something you love, why not share what you've learnt with others and become a guitar teacher (for example) for younger kids yourself?

Aged 12, I had four success stories (which was great for marketing) and enough money to visit the cinema as many times as I liked.

There are a few lessons that we could all learn from 12-year-old me:

1. Challenge yourself. Despite being dyslexic I chose to teach other students English. I worked

on my weaknesses (i.e., working on my spelling in my spare time), and I wasn't afraid to get things wrong.

2. Understand that there is value in what you do. I could have chosen to provide my tuition services at no cost. While that would have been admirable, it would have left me out of pocket, and, in the long term, I would have been unhappy. This lesson doesn't mean that you shouldn't do things for free; instead, see this as a way of being of service while knowing your worth.

3. Embrace your unique ideas, even if they seem risky and disruptive. At 12 years old I took a risk and disrupted the tuition market. I wasn't afraid to embrace my unique and daring idea of bringing down the cost of tuition to a point where my competitors simply couldn't deliver a better value proposition.

If you believe that you have a unique skill or passion that you think could be monetized, don't be afraid to start a business. I delivered group tuition classes from my parents' living room throughout my secondary school years and for the duration of both of my degrees. By the age of 18, I was teaching 50+ students in group sessions every weekend. I learnt the art of delegation and roped in my brothers to deliver the Mathematics and Non-Verbal Reasoning tuition. This allowed me to focus on building my strengths in English and Verbal Reasoning. With my parents' support, I ran one of North London's leading tuition centres from their living room.

I strive to be innovative in business, and I credit my dyslexia for this, as I do believe that it changes my creative thinking. As well as having made me resilient, my different brain is good at thinking "outside the box" and having innovative ideas. My primary goal in business has always been to have maximum reach, and it became clear that my parents' living room couldn't meet the high demand for my tuition services. So, in my third year of university, after spending some time studying Online Education in China, I took the tuition services online, moved into the EdTech space, and built what is now known as **Enrich Learning**. I have always had an interest in online education and knew that I would be able to serve a greater number of students online because one of the benefits of a digital offering is access to a wider, borderless, international audience.

I write about Enrich Learning with so much pride now, but for a long time this was not the case. I hid my business from the general public until the age of 19, when I had my first international press feature. I thought it was quite unbelievable that a black dyslexic woman could successfully run a business in the education sector, despite the fact that I was doing this. I've mentioned my inner critic earlier! As I also mentioned earlier, I had been shown dyslexic entrepreneurs in the past, but **none** who looked remotely like me. This meant that I felt like a bit of a fraud or an imposter. I did, however, gain the confidence to unapologetically showcase my business by the time I was in my early twenties. This confidence grew when I decided that I would be the representation the world so clearly lacks.

Since going public about Enrich Learning, I have gone from strength to strength. I have been featured in a wide range of publications, including American business magazine, *Forbes*. The business has grown and now serves a wide range of people across the world, including those in the neurodivergent community. Most importantly, more children, young people and families have come to know about Enrich Learning and the most incredible success that has come through students using our online education platform.

Building Enrich Learning has been one of the greatest honours of my life. Seeing the positive difference it has made in my community and beyond has been uplifting, and I am beyond grateful to 12-year-old me who was fearless in her pursuit of making her dreams a reality. In sharing the Enrich Learning story with you, I hope you are encouraged to take a leap of faith and create your own destiny. Don't sit on your ideas – endeavour to enact them. I say this because carrying out my ideas helped me cope during the most testing times of my life. Like most, if not all, teenagers, I had challenging moments, but having my business gave me hope. Your stimulus doesn't have to be business; it can be whatever you wish. All I ask is that you do not allow your difference to hold you back.

Chapter 6

#FFE312

If you asked me to describe the first five years of my secondary schooling, I would give you three words: challenging, complex, character-building. Even after completing two degrees, I still see those formative academic years of my life as some of the most difficult yet enjoyable times I will ever experience. I initially (and naively) thought that my diagnosis would unlock the gates to happiness and authenticity. To some degree, it did. I was able to have a better understanding of myself, which is a good thing for any teenager. My parents and teachers were able to give me the tailored support required to help me maximize my potential. This enabled me to use my talents effectively, giving me a much-needed confidence boost. My initial reflections on life as a dyslexic teen were positive, although it must be said that there were significant negative periods too.

I had to deal with relentless bullying from some pupils, which made me fearful and grossly unhappy. I was constantly worried about disappointing my parents – they had given up so much in their lives to enable me to have the best possible education, and I felt I had let them down by being dyslexic. I had to find new, unconventional ways of learning. It took me a while to understand and accept that I was different to my peers. For the first couple of years post diagnosis, I was ashamed of my difference and desperately wanted to be like everyone else.

The bullying started when Mrs G recommended I use an overlay to read and/or to use yellow paper (shade #FFE312 specifically). I remember distinctly asking her what an overlay was and why I needed one. An overlay is a coloured filter that is used to alleviate reading difficulties that are associated with learning disabilities, including dyslexia. The magic happens when you place the thin, coloured plastic sheet over text – it stops the words from floating around on a stark white page. In order to find the colour that would work for me specifically, Mrs G ran a test on me. She had a paragraph, with little to no line spacing, and the content of the paragraph was the same sentence repeated several times. It read: "The quick brown fox jumps over the lazy dog." Every test I did in order to confirm that I am dyslexic revolved around this sentence. There is a reason for this – it is an English pangram, meaning that it contains all of the letters of the English alphabet.

Mrs G asked me to read the paragraph out loud while using different coloured overlays. We began with a beautiful shade of lilac; this helped to some degree, but I was still stumbling over some of the words. Mrs G then switched to a light green; this made matters worse. She then placed a rose-pink overlay over the paragraph and there was some improvement; but the eureka moment took place when she placed a deep golden yellow overlay on the page. Everything became clear, my reading was fluent and my reading speed increased. For the first time in my life the words were not playing tricks on me. It was a special moment. Mrs G gave me the sample overlay to use and took her time to make me my very own overlays. She knew that I would end up forgetting to take one to every class, so she made enough for me to keep one in every folder. Mrs G taught me to keep life simple by putting processes in place to help me not just survive, but to thrive.

Mrs G suggested that in subjects such as English, History and Religious Studies, my teachers should print out my resources on the very bright yellow paper as this would help me...and it did. It helped me massively. In my first year of secondary school, I achieved a grade C in my end of year English exam. In my second year, where I had consistently used a coloured filter or coloured paper, I didn't just achieve an A*; I received the highest mark in my year and was awarded with the English Literature prize. It's a common misconception that dyslexic people are bad at English Literature, but this simply isn't the case. With the right support in place, the Arts and Humanities may be a dyslexic person's academic strength. I became so good at writing that I have been able to write the book that you're now reading. Some deemed my academic success unlikely, but I was able to exceed expectations against all the odds.

The overlays and yellow paper were incredible, but when you have a bright yellow plastic sheet sticking out of every folder, or even worse, when you have to place this plastic sheet over a piece of paper that you're sharing with your classmates, you inevitably become a target. When you accidentally drop a bright piece of yellow paper on the ground and you're the only child in the school that uses that specific shade, all 800+ students know that it's yours. I became a bit of a laughing stock for some of the pupils. There were sniggers and giggles when I pulled out my overlay, eye rolls and grunts when I would place the overlay on a sheet of paper in group tasks, and a continuous game of 21 questions when the teacher had forgotten to prepare my yellow sheets before the class had started and needed to pop down to the photocopier room. It was exhausting. Like most teens, I just wanted to be liked, and I felt that the overlay was stopping some of my peers from liking me.

Matters became worse when it was discovered

that I struggle to read green ink on a whiteboard. Mrs G ensured that my teachers were informed of this privately via email. They politely asked my teachers that, when they were teaching me, they should refrain from using the green whiteboard pen. Following the low-level bullying I was already experiencing from using a coloured overlay or coloured paper, I hoped that my teachers would not bring the issue up in front of the class. I trusted that they would acknowledge the email and cease using the green pen. My trust was immediately broken when one teacher loudly explained on my arrival into class that they had received an email that I couldn't see green because I have dyslexia. The email had been sent out the day before. Not only did this teacher misinterpret what was said, but their well-intentioned exclamation also meant that my entire class knew about what I'll call "the green issue" and I couldn't even have peace for 24 hours. I was flooded with questions from my peers – some of them genuine, some of them spiteful. All I wanted to do was leave the class to cry. That specific lesson was not one of my favourite subjects – I strongly disliked the subject because my brain just couldn't (and still can't) get to grips with how it worked. My dislike for it was now exacerbated by my teacher's unintentional mistake in revealing "the green issue".

 Let's briefly explore this. My issue with green pen on a whiteboard is likened to scotopic sensitivity syndrome (SSS), which is also known as Meares-Irlen syndrome/Irlen syndrome. SSS is the experience of unpleasant visual symptoms when reading, especially for prolonged periods of time. The green pen on the whiteboard distressed me beyond measure. For starters, I couldn't actually read what was written, and when I could, I would concentrate so hard that I would give myself headaches. In other words, the green pen on the whiteboard over-stimulated my brain, which caused me discomfort. This discomfort was stopping me from learning. When Mrs G discovered that the answer was to stop using the green pen, it seemed like a quick, easy and simple solution. It's important to note that SSS is quite common for dyslexic people but it is often overlooked It shouldn't be, because being able to concentrate is essential for everyone and anyone who wants to learn.

Many teachers simply couldn't get their heads

around why they shouldn't use green pen on the whiteboard when I was in class. Some publicly moaned about it, which encouraged my peers to mock me further. I cannot describe to you how much this hurt. Being constantly ridiculed forced me to lie about my condition. I told my teachers and peers that I was colour-blind so that they would leave me alone. I thought that would make matters better, but it did the complete opposite, and made matters worse. I was forever explaining myself, which was both tiresome and tedious.

My feelings were not initially visible to the staff. My pain manifested into an uncontrollable anxiety, which left me with irritable bowel syndrome (IBS), a condition I am still learning to cope with now, as an adult. I found comfort in Matron's Office (especially when Matron P was on duty). I think Matron P recognized that my repeated upset stomach wasn't because I had eaten something funny. After all, in a boarding school, we all eat the same thing – if the food was dodgy, the entire boarding house would have the runs. Matron P would often talk to me about how and why I worried. Now I know that the majority of my worries were tied to being dyslexic. When I was a teenager, I couldn't see this because I had not yet developed the emotional intelligence that would have helped me have a greater understanding of myself and my feelings. My dyslexia knocked my self-esteem; it made me develop a crippling anxiety that affected my physical and mental health. Many neurodivergent teenagers will experience this and, in sharing my story, I hope awareness is raised about this, as no teen should suffer in the way that I did.

The teachers at my school could see that something was troubling me, and at one point I was given therapy sessions that really did help me. The most effective was the weekly private neuro-linguistic programming (NLP) sessions I had with the new head of Teaching and Learning, who I'm going to call Mr Zen, because no matter how frantic I appeared, he always had a way of restoring calm.

In our NLP sessions I learnt how to visualize positivity. This seems like an odd concept, but allow me to explain. Generally speaking, dyslexic people are brilliant at visualizing. This means that they are really good at forming a mental image of something, ranging from a creative idea, to what might happen in the future. Mr Zen spotted early on in our relationship that I had a habit of visualizing the worst possible outcome in everything that I did. This meant that I worked myself up and created a dreadful cloud of worry that physically and mentally hung over me in my early years of secondary education.

The first thing Mr Zen worked on was teaching me how to re-frame my mind. He encouraged me to identify the thoughts, feelings and behaviours I wanted to change. Sometimes I would write these thoughts and feelings out, but our sessions were mostly oral, because that is what I felt most comfortable doing. I was taught how to establish contact with the innermost part of myself, and I began to discover what was triggering the negative moods. It was (and still is, at times) fear. I was fearful of failing academically, despite having never failed at anything I had done. I maintained excellent grades throughout school, but genuinely thought that I was stupid. In our NLP sessions, I was forced to ask myself **why** I felt this way. My feelings stemmed from my Nigerian heritage.

Education is massively important in Nigerian culture, and Igbo people are especially passionate about it, with the common belief being that education is the key to success. Being a lover of literature and enthusiast of education, I put myself under undue pressure to be the best. I wanted to be like Chinua Achebe and Chimamanda Ngozi Adichie, two Igbo heroes who have led the way in literature. I wanted to be an excellent example to my brothers by having great grades. Everything was about my grades. My obsessive nature towards my studies was unhealthy and unproductive. Mr Zen worked hard to help me understand that my academic accolades did not define me – my grades were simply part of who I was. I also learnt that my academic journey was a marathon and not a sprint. Being a great visualizer meant that I would often focus on the big picture and the end goal. The end goal varied from getting the top marks in my year in English (my favourite subject) to getting to grips with understanding simultaneous equations. I would get frustrated about having to go through the process of getting there.

I now have a handful of practical tips I use:

1. Plan. I've said it before, and I'll say it again. This time my focus is on planning **how** you will reach that end goal. Mr Zen and I would produce weekly plans with specific steps on what I needed to do, which would enable me to actualize the big picture I had created in my mind. For example, if I had to submit an essay, we would break down the steps of what needed to be done to write it. I would review each step as I went along the planned journey. This would take the pressure off.

2. Give yourself extra time. Mr Zen noticed that it took me longer than other pupils to complete tasks that he asked me to do in our sessions. He and Mrs G applied for me to have 25% extra time in all my exams. This helped massively. It allowed me to focus on the task at hand and, to some extent, to take my eyes off the clock. This eased my anxiety – the IBS flare-ups became infrequent. If you're unsure about how to get extra time, speak to a schoolteacher or university lecturer as soon as you possibly can – the application process for extra time can be lengthy and complicated. You may require a diagnosis

for it, which would mean completing a full dyslexia assessment.

3. Talk. I'm a chatty person by nature, so this step wasn't hard for me. Putting that aside, encouraging a dyslexic person to speak about how they feel is important. Until my sessions with Mr Zen, I felt hopeless. I constantly felt as if I was failing, when the truth was, that in many ways, I was thriving. I just needed to understand this as well as be reminded that I was working in a neurotypical environment while being a neurodivergent person. Schools aren't generally built for people like me, so I had to be kind to myself while making adjustments in order to learn efficiently and effectively.

My sessions with Mr Zen were great because I learnt how to get to know myself. I built skills that helped me to become reflective. I discovered that dyslexia comes with great talents, such as being able to visualize the entire picture in a holistic way. I developed strategies that made my anxiety almost non-existent. It was incredible. The only thing Mr Zen could not do was control the actions of other children. I worked on myself extensively, but that didn't stop some of them from being unnecessarily cruel to me.

What I have come to see as the bullying became unbearable one summer. I had begun to really enjoy using social media. I had used it to lead on the #BringBackOurGirls campaign and gained some celebrity traction, which was exciting. During the summer, pupils kept in touch via various forms of social media. It was the first time that many of us had been given permission to have a social media account. The way in which we used it was mostly harmless, although we had admittedly not yet learnt the etiquette of how to behave online. Most kids were kind to each other, but with very little education about to use social media appropriately, it was inevitable that some unkind comments would be exchanged between teens.

There was a conversation regarding African foods, and because I am of Nigerian, more specifically, Igbo, heritage, naturally I wanted to join in. Anyone who knows me well will testify that my love of food is somewhat all-consuming; however, I often have a hard time ordering Nigerian dishes because I can never spell or say them correctly. While I can read, write, speak and fluently understand the language, I have never been able to fully grasp the letters and the sounds. Igbo delicacies include: ogbono, ofe nsala, onugbu, nkwobi, okro and ukwa. I challenge you to read that list aloud and first, work out how you think the words should sound. Second, ask yourself whether these dishes sound anything like how they are spelt. Third, imagine this being your everyday experience – something as simple as texting your mother what you would like for dinner becomes a rather tiresome affair.

Despite my nervousness around spelling these dishes correctly, I still wanted to get stuck into the debate, and I did. Understandably, while getting involved with the conversation I spelt the name of a dish incorrectly. My peers paid no attention to this spelling mistake, except for one child, who went on to make what I felt to be a rather unkind comment. Within minutes my peers, who had previously paid my spelling mistake no mind, were now commenting about it across various different social media platforms. I'll admit that I didn't make matters better by arguing that I had spelt the dish correctly because my mother, who is also dyslexic, said I had. On reflection, I was hopelessly trying to stick up for myself. I had had enough of repeatedly being the joke of the day. A few hours passed and I fearfully explained that I was dyslexic, which means that I was not very good at spelling. My explanation fell on deaf ears. What I found to be personally very upsetting bullying spiralled out of control. Luckily I had enough courage to show my parents who immediately contacted my school for a resolution. If you ever feel as if you are being bullied and would prefer to speak to someone removed from the situation, I encourage you to ring ChildLine on 0800 1111.

The dreaded start to my "Great Erasmus year" (you may be more familiar with the term "Year 11" (age 15–16) – my school had its own name for everything) came quickly. I was not looking forward to it at all, and my dismay was not because I had GCSE exams to sit; my dismay was fuelled by the fear of having to face up to "the bullying". My parents insisted that we go and see the deputy heads, and I eventually agreed because the cons of being called a "snitch" outweighed the horrors of being bullied. I just wanted it to stop. We sat before two staff members, one of them admitting they were new to the job. I'll be honest, I had little faith that these teachers, despite being members of the school's senior management, could do anything to help me. I had lived through this bullying for **years** and it had gone unnoticed. One of the deputy heads had even taught me English for a year but had still failed to recognize what was going on behind the scenes. How could an issue that had gone on for so long be resolved in a 30-minute meeting? Little did I know that having a fresh pair of eyes, the eyes of the new deputy head, take a look at my situation would be surprisingly helpful.

My use of the word "surprisingly" here is intentional. Our new deputy head – I'm going to call him Mr Honourable – was unbelievably rational. Perhaps I had been subjected to such irrational and extensive bullying that it had clouded my sense of judgement. The bullying made me think that the way I was being treated was both normal and acceptable. The thought that matters could be resolved seemed a distant dream. Unlike previous attempts to solve the bullying issue, which, in short, was various teachers having "conversations" with unkind students, Mr Honourable only wanted the facts. He wasn't interested in my dyslexia because, quite frankly, having a learning difference wasn't a reason to be bullied. He cut through the bitchiness that comes with girl-on-girl bullying, and immediately came up with a solution. The bullies were to be suspended from school, thus ending this matter.

My initial thoughts about involving an entirely new member of staff in this situation were wrong. I thought he simply wouldn't understand my situation, but he did. He understood it because, unlike many of my other teachers, he knew that being resilient was great, but **everyone** had a breaking point. And I had hit mine. By the time we had come to the deputy heads with the bullying problem, I had such low self-esteem that it was exacerbating my IBS and it was hard to imagine how I would make it to the end of the meeting without quite literally shitting myself.

Let's talk about the harsh realities of bullying that are often overlooked. Bullying creates trauma that can cause life-disrupting consequences. In my case, it has caused my bowels to have a bit of wobble every time I have the slightest feeling of anxiety or doubt. For others, bullying can cause depression that brings such low moods the person being bullied loses the ability to function. Neurodivergent people are more likely to experience bullying because society does not accept or celebrate difference. I, like many other dyslexic children, was bullied because I am different. The bullies didn't like or appreciate my difference, and instead ridiculed me, which left me feeling ashamed of who I was.

What hurt the most is that the bullying was mostly carried out by girls. Girl-on-girl bullying comes with a cult-like cattiness, which means that not only is the victim being treated badly, but they are also excluded from other social groups, leaving them isolated and alone. I was lucky to have the support of my best friend, however, who completely disassociated herself from such a toxic environment – the bullying just went over her head. Our friendship was (and still is) my saving grace.

You may be reading this as someone who has

experienced bullying because, like me, you're different. First and foremost, I encourage you to speak out. If you're being bullied, whether at school, at home or in the office, you **must** tell someone. I urge you to celebrate your difference and to seek friendships with those who accept you for who you are. You may also be reading this as someone who is presently playing the role of bully, or who has played that role in the past. I implore you to recognize that you hurt people because you are a hurt person yourself. Then I encourage you to take steps to heal your pain so that you can #bekind.

Mr Honourable played an invaluable role in helping me recover and move forward from the episodes of bullying that I had experienced. Interestingly, he didn't make any mention of my dyslexia. He didn't ignore it, but I think he recognized that the focus on it distracted staff from helping me escape the bullies. Before his arrival at the school, I had been encouraged to "bounce back", "be strong" and "be resilient". These are all great messages, but they shouldn't come as a result of continual bullying. Mr Honourable made it very clear to me that being dyslexic was not a reason for someone to be bullied.

He helped me understand that characteristics like resilience can be built without the suffering that comes with being bullied. It was the first time I had accepted that I wasn't to be blamed for the unkind actions of others. Mr Honourable taught me that I could build characteristics like resilience in my extra-curricular activities. He helped me see that I could have a life outside of academic study. I learnt to have hobbies that showcased my strengths. I began to build an enriched life outside of the classroom.

Let's start with debating. I've already mentioned how I'm a bit of a chatterbox – I love to talk about everything and anything. More importantly, I love to argue (in a constructive way). For three years Mr Honourable coached me on how to debate. I went from being a bit of a rambler to being able to concisely and sharply argue my case in front of a crowd. I got really good at debating and went on to become the vice president of the Debating Society as well as an Oxford Schools Finalist. Debating empowered me to speak up, speak out and speak authentically. It gave me voice (and a bit of "cool" factor). The kids who used to tease me wanted to become my friend. If there was a class debate, rather than being the last person to be picked to join a group, I was the first. Debating gave me a sense of belonging.

The skills I picked up in debating enabled me to join the Model United Nations (MUN) at school, which, at the time, was selected by the teachers and was therefore "exclusive". What I mean by this is that staff handpicked students to join the MUN. Members of the MUN were considered intelligent, so being picked to take part really boosted my confidence. I climbed the ranks, and in my final year of school I was secretary-general. I won an award at every MUN conference I attended and, most importantly, I built up a huge amount of self-belief. Taking part in these activities helped me learn how to build relationships with other people and stopped me from living in isolation.

If there are opportunities at school or at work that you think may help with your self-development, whether it's a council for making environmentally friendly changes in your school, creating a network/ community in the office or joining the debating society, or some other school/work club, don't shy away from them because you have a learning difference. Instead, my advice would be to take yourself out of your comfort zone and to participate.

I also developed an interest in writing. In my English classes I would go above and beyond in my homework – if I was asked to write two pages, I would submit three. I developed a good relationship with the school librarian who always ordered the new books I requested. I found myself, aged 15, discussing the Booker Prize entries with my English teacher. I had found my passion. The head of the English Department was massively supportive and took time out of his busy schedule to read my creative pieces of work. He noticed that I had a talent and would give me tutorials, where I learnt how to write well.

Here are some of the tips I picked up:

1. Read, read, read! I know dyslexic people find reading hard because sometimes the words move about on the page. Get an assessment done (with an educational psychologist), find out if

you need an overlay and get reading. Remember that you can read in different ways. Audiobooks are a great alternative. Do whatever makes it easier for you to engage with literature.

2. Keep stress levels low. When I'm stressed, none of my sentences make sense. Stress makes dyslexia symptoms worse. Writing should be fun, so when you're spending time with a pen and paper or with your fingers tapping away on a keyboard, do so in a stress-free environment. Aromatherapy is a simple and effective stress reliever – I often have a mildly scented candle burning while I write.

3. Practise writing frequently. I write every day. Every tweet, Instagram caption, LinkedIn post and WhatsApp message is a form of writing. There are some days when I produce phenomenal work and some days when the work is, quite frankly, rubbish. It doesn't matter because practice will help you create the very best version of your work. I will not use the saying "Practice makes perfect" because perfectionism will hold you back. Just write.

4. Give yourself plenty of time. Dyslexic people tend to have slower processing speeds, meaning that we need extra time to complete tasks. Accept that it will take you longer to write and be okay with that. You'll get there eventually.

5. Share your writing with people (and don't be disheartened when the feedback isn't positive). My head of English was happy to read and mark my extra work. Sometimes his feedback was harsh – when a piece of work didn't read well, he wasn't afraid to say so. His feedback showed me what I needed to work on. Taking his directives on board enabled me to get very good at writing. At the end of Year 11 I was awarded an English Scholarship for my sixth form study. This would not have been possible without his continuous feedback.

The confidence I built in my GCSE years empowered me to choose to complete the International Baccalaureate (IB) Diploma Programme instead of A-Levels for my sixth form study. The IB is an assessed programme for students aged 16–19. In order to complete it, you must study at least two languages, a Humanities-based subject, Mathematics, a science and what the IB calls "Theory of Knowledge". My subject choices included: English Literature, History, Philosophy, French, Biology and Maths Studies as well as the compulsory Theory of Knowledge programme.

My parents, and some teachers, were rather nervous about my decision to take on what was a significantly challenging programme for my sixth form study. I had spent my secondary school years coping with stress and anxiety. The people who cared about me deeply were worried that I had picked a programme that would be out of my depth. I'll honestly admit that I wanted to prove to everyone, and most importantly, to myself, that I was just as, if not more, academic than my peers. Being dyslexic didn't stop me from taking the more challenging academic option. The IB allowed me to explore without constraints, which, I believe, was much better for me, and one of the ways I cope with my dyslexia. I'll give you an example to illustrate what I mean.

The IB English Literature course gave students

the option to choose what they wanted to study. For example, I was given the opportunity to study African-American short stories in great detail instead of 19th-century English poetry. I love poetry and had spent a lot of time in school studying it. I didn't want to limit myself to what I knew, so I studied African-American literature instead. My A-Level peers were not afforded such a choice – they were restricted to texts on the syllabus list. I knew in my heart that I would not have enjoyed studying in that way.

The IB also had a focus on service – there was a compulsory community service requirement. Students had to be proactive in helping out in their communities. I completed my community service at Queen Elizabeth II Silver Jubilee School in Horsham. For two years I spent one afternoon a week supporting children with severe and profound multiple special needs. The needs of the pupils at the school were vast, with some children needing physical, medical and sensory support. This experience is something that I will never forget, and it was this part of the IB programme that showed me the importance of service.

The children looked forward to every visit I made to the school. Some didn't understand the activities that we did, but I could see in their eyes that they appreciated every moment. I began to understand that I must lead my life with a focus on service because your service determines your greatness. Prior to my community service activity, I didn't believe that I could be of service to another child because I am dyslexic. I worried when I had to read aloud to the children. I feared stumbling over my words. The truth is that the children never noticed when I did miss a word out of a sentence, and when they did, we just laughed about it. By being of service, I learnt that in order to be kind to others, I had to be kind to myself. By being of service, I was able to see how dyslexia could not stop me from helping others.

All in all, the IB taught me how to juggle many plates at one time effortlessly. At the start of the course, I had found it hard to keep up. I'm sure I spent the first week or two running from one class to another – a bit like when I started school aged 11. You may be wondering why I reflect on this with such gladness. It's because completing the IB taught me how to

get comfortable with being uncomfortable. I was thrown in at the deep end, and at times it felt like I was drowning.

The important thing is that I learnt how to face up to my fears in a fearless manner. Of course, I would have appreciated having a slightly lighter workload, but all teenagers wish for this to be the case. There were weeks when I had three 2,000-word essays due. I would write all day (and sometimes all night). I didn't mind working so hard because the work allowed me to read, read, read, and to practise writing frequently. Nothing, however, could have better prepared me for university.

Chapter 7

From Kensington Olympia to London Waterloo

I started thinking about university a year before my peers. I would spend my free time looking at various university websites with a focus on their special educational needs provision. It was always possible to find what measures universities put in place to ensure that neurodivergent students thrived in such academic environments. I eventually came across King's College London (KCL), which was better than most institutions in the sense that it was relatively easy to discover the offering for dyslexic students like me. This was dependent on how proactive the student was, but I guess that this is the significant difference between university and school – at university you have to be willing to do things without prompts and reminders!

At this point it's important that I share a harsh reality about the university application process. Going to a top university may not be the best thing for neurodivergent people. When I was in Year 12 (age 16–17), for a period of time I had my heart set on reading Theology at an Oxbridge College. I had entered an essay competition where I was commended and invited for tea by the College administrators. My dad and I had a private tour. While we were there, we had a meeting with the College tutors to discuss what measures could be put in place to help me cope with the academic rigor and my dyslexia. While we had a lovely day, and the College staff were wonderfully kind, deep down I knew I would struggle to maximize my potential in the environment I had been shown. I was told that I would be expected to hand in multiple thousand-word essays a week and manage a heavy reading load in what was a considerably short academic term in comparison to other universities (Oxbridge runs on eight teaching weeks per term; other universities typically run on 10–12 teaching weeks). The stress that I would have had to learn to cope with would have been bad for both my physical and mental health.

I felt as if I was also discouraged from working while studying, which greatly concerned me. I wanted to continue building my business while at university. Entrepreneurship gave me something else to focus on – it stopped me from becoming obsessive about my academic performance. Running my own business also meant that I could support myself financially while at university. There is nothing worse than having money worries while trying to study. The challenge of not being able to live comfortably would make anyone grossly unhappy. It was clear that my dream of attending Oxbridge for university was not in my best interests. This was a hard truth pill to swallow.

It is important that we all have realistic expectations of what we can handle, but this doesn't mean that we stop dreaming big. I'm a dreamer, and I have created a lot of my own success, but I'm also a realist, which means that I have a good understanding of what my threshold is. Ensure that you know what you can tolerate. I knew that I wouldn't be able to cope being a broke student, trying to study in a high-pressured environment – and that's okay.

I decided to go ahead and apply for a place, but I did so for the experience rather than for the hope of actually attending Oxbridge for university. This may seem rather odd, but the process of making the application made my personal statement so much better than what it would have been had I not made an Oxbridge application. I drafted my personal statement seven times, had too many meetings with my personal tutor to discuss it, and ensured that it was as good as it could possibly be. It turned out to be the best decision I had made in my academic life.

I had offers to read Theology/Religion, Politics and Society from King's College London, Durham University, the University of Exeter and the University of Edinburgh, some of the very best universities in the world. The Oxbridge college application was a stepping-stone to gaining admission at one of the best Theology and Religious

Studies departments in the world – King's College London (KCL). If the Theology and Religious Studies department at KCL was good enough for Noble Peace Laureate Archbishop Desmond Tutu, then it was certainly good enough for me.

Being dyslexic has meant that I almost always go the extra mile. This includes always having to leave home several hours before I need to arrive at a location because I have to factor in enough time for getting lost. As a university student it meant spending multiple hours attending meetings with lecturers because I didn't understand a concept that had been taught in the lecture room, because the lecturer had gone over it too quickly. I am really grateful to those lecturers for the extra time they spent clarifying concepts with me. If you are a dyslexic student yourself, my advice would be, do ask if you don't understand something because the lecture went too fast or for any other reason. You are your own best advocate to explain your dyslexia to your teachers, and at university your lecturers are there to support you and your learning process! Being dyslexic as a student also meant missing nights out to be in the library writing essays, because it took me longer than my peers to complete my assignments.

 When I decided that KCL was the university for me, I didn't just attend the open day. I wrote to the head of the Theology and Religious Studies department and arranged to have a private meeting with a lecturer who gave me more details about the course I was applying for, as well as what student life looked like in the middle of London. This was massively eye-opening because not only did I discover the various different modules, but it also became quite clear that I would have to get to grips with, quite literally, walking from one end of London to another in between lectures. I would recommend you do this too if like me you can struggle with journeys and navigation, and because as a dyslexic, you are going to have a lot more to consider and it is good to know as much about your course and university as you can in advance.

The lecturer explained that there would be times where I would have to walk across Waterloo Bridge to get to the Strand, I would have to navigate my way from the Strand to the Kingsway-

Holborn (the Theology and Religious Studies department building), and, in my final year, add in the destination of Bush House. In other words, I would have to learn to love Google Maps (I don't like Citymapper). This may seem insignificant to you, but for a dyslexic person, navigation is really important because the stress of trying to find a location can exacerbate symptoms, leaving them unable to study efficiently. I'll admit that when I first started university, trying to get around a campus that is quite literally spread out across London was challenging. I also had to commute in from South East London, which was hard, considering my secondary school commute had been a 5-minute walk or cycle from my bedroom to the classroom.

Once I got my head around maps and directions, then came the all-important issue of managing my dyslexia. Unsurprisingly the lecturers in my department had little knowledge about dyslexia support at KCL. Following my meeting, I was given an email address, a random URL to check out and a massive dose of encouragement to sort things out **before** term started. The summer before my first university term was filled with emails going back and forth between myself and numerous staff members trying to see what needed to be done to ensure that I continued to receive extra time in assessments and that my examination materials were printed on #FFE312 (yellow) paper. I was eventually directed to Disability Support, which informed me that before any support plans could be put in place, I would need to do another assessment with an educational psychologist. It was implied that I might no longer need the support described above because I was over the age of 18.

The repeated assessments that educational institutions require dyslexic students to go through seem to imply that dyslexia can "stop" or "disappear" and to me, this seemed at the time quite bizarre. Let me make something clear – dyslexia is a lifelong condition, with no cure. Luckily there are plenty of resources to help with the management of dyslexia, but the support needed is life long. As an adult with a greater understanding of dyslexia I can see that what they meant to say is that a re-assessment is needed once a dyslexic person becomes an adult, because their needs may have changed. I wholeheartedly agree with this and think it is important that this is made clear to people with learning differences when the repeat assessments happen.

My assessment took place in mid-August just after my 18th birthday. I was very anxious, had a sleepless night and worst of all, wasn't sure about the location. I left home 3 hours before my appointment despite only living an hour away from the KCL campus. My efforts seemed to have been in vain because I was still late. There were several train cancellations, I had gone to the wrong station and found myself walking between different KCL campus buildings trying to find my assessment room. The educational psychologist who conducted my assessment commented on my lateness. I was too tired and upset to explain my problems with the journey, and tears formed behind my eyes. I was probably feeling extra sensitive because of the long tortuous journey, but I didn't bother to explain myself as I didn't want to risk aggravating them further. From their point of view, I was late to the assessment and they had other things to do that day. As a busy person myself, I can understand their frustration but think it's important for all of us to recognize that being dyslexic affects various aspects of a person's life – including timings.

The assessment was similar to what I had had as a child, but it took an awfully long time to complete it. Until now, I almost felt as if the purpose of it was to tire me out. The assessor ended our meeting by stating that they needed seven working days to draw up their conclusions. I really appreciate the incredibly in-depth assessment in retrospect, but at the time, I felt strange after the assessment. The wait felt long and I wasn't sure whether it meant I was in a weird purgatory for not having been diagnosed as having dyslexia (as it seemed as though my dyslexic status had expired) but I was still having dyslexic symptoms. Ten days later as I recall (because university admin is **always** late), a 29-page report was emailed to me confirming that I was, indeed, a dyslexic adult with a range of needs that university staff must support in order for me to thrive at KCL.

When I reflect on my adult dyslexia assessment, I'm grateful for a number of reasons. The first is that KCL saved me £800+. I can forgive what I felt to be the university's occasional lack of administrative efficiency when they saved me such a significant amount of money. Adult special educational needs assessments are grossly expensive. These much-needed assessments are inaccessible and unaffordable. Had I not been proactive and asked the university about what I could do to help myself, I know that I would have ended up taking the assessment privately, and spending a fortune in the process.

For those of you who are looking to get an adult assessment for dyslexia without spending an arm and a leg, here are a few tips:

1. If you work for company, have a conversation with human resources (HR) and see if they can help you source funding for your assessment. The company may be able to pay for the assessment or may be linked to organizations that can deliver the assessment at a reduced cost.

2. If you're unsure about whether you have dyslexia, but you recognize that you have the

154 | Dyslexia and Me

symptoms, do a screening test before you attend a full assessment. A dyslexia screening test is an affordable way of confirming that you have the genuine signs of dyslexia.

3. Contact your local dyslexia association – you can find out where yours is via the British Dyslexia Association website. These are run by dedicated volunteers who are experienced in finding people the very best, most accessible, support.

At KCL what I found was that the university was great in that, where they can support a student with learning differences, they will, but **the students have to find the support for themselves**. I am bold and courageous by nature, so finding the support I needed was second nature to me. However, many students are shy and would struggle to email people they have never met before. Many, whatever their personality trait, wouldn't even know where to start, though I hope my story in this book might give them some ideas. In my opinion, universities need to make special educational needs information readily available. Universities need to play an active role in promoting the various special education needs/learning difference awareness days, weeks and months that have been put into our calendars. Universities need to run campaigns to increase the visibility of learning differences. Universities must make greater efforts to celebrate neurodivergence.

I settled into my first year of university fairly well. Having completed the IB meant that there was no amount of workload that I could not cope with. I had come from a place where the weekly expectation was a submission of 6,000 words in the form of essays; at KCL, my 6,000-word submissions were expected by the end of the term. I felt that I had been given a moment to catch my breath, which was much appreciated. A King's Inclusion Plan (KIP) was developed for me. This explained what my needs were and how the lecturers could best support me. I was also given a support worker, who I was given the opportunity to meet with when I wanted to review my KIP and make changes if and when necessary. Part of my KIP included a coversheet, which I attached to all pieces of assessed work. This instructed markers to take into account my dyslexia. It explained that my spelling may be inconsistent and my sentences may be incoherent. This was great because it meant that markers couldn't mark me down for the odd mistake. Of course, my work was always held to the highest standard, but the coversheet made it clear that I was working with challenges that many of my peers simply did not have.

In general, things started off well, and my overall experience at King's was incredible, with brilliant accommodations made for me in exams, as you'll see as you read on. However, there was one horrid experience that I'll never forget, and want to write about here to show you the kind of thing that can go wrong for dyslexics anywhere, in case it reminds you, whether you are an educator or a student yourself, that you can never do too much advance planning and emailing, to be absolutely sure that a dyslexic student's needs are met...!

It was a wet, cold, gloomy January morning. I was getting ready to attend my mandatory Study Skills module exam. All students were told that **all** KCL exams were to take place in the halls of Kensington Olympia. From the beginning, this was incredibly challenging for me. Having finally gotten my head around the Waterloo to Strand to Kingsway (Holborn) journey, I had to add in the complicated journey of going from New Cross Gate to Kensington Olympia. Getting across South London was like completing an assault course to me, with multiple train changes and limited bus routes.

On the day of my Study Skills exam (which was more like an adult spelling, punctuation and grammar assessment), I consciously made the decision not to eat for fear of an IBS episode. I left the house with my flatmate-turned-lifetime-friend (who I'm going to call H), and we made the journey to the exam location. H, like me, had a fear of being late and getting lost. It was our first exam at university, and we wanted to make a good impression. We left the house with 2 hours travel time when Google Maps told us we only needed one.

When we arrived at Kensington Olympia, we were shocked to be met by thousands of KCL students, pushing and shoving their way into the building. I swallowed a huge gulp of anxiety, and, with clammy hands (caused by anxiety sweat), I made my way to the seat allocation board. I saw my name in bold: **"Onyinyewchukwu Udokporo – Waterloo Campus"**. I thought I was in a bad dream. I rubbed my eyes and looked again, only to find that my allocated seat for the exam was on the other side of South London, at the KCL Waterloo campus. I didn't want to cry as my entire year group was there, but my heart broke as I had to face the reality of potentially failing my first ever exam at university. In that moment, I had convinced myself that the university had made an admin error and meant to give me a seat at Olympia. I ignored the problem and went off to join my classmates.

The worst thing for me about the Olympia set-up was that everyone used it as an opportunity to quiz their friends about what they knew just before an exam. I cannot tell you just how unhelpful this is for everyone involved. Let's face it, there are some people who will ask you things before an exam simply to catch you out. Students have oddly disguised this rather toxic habit as "last-minute revision". I don't think there is such a thing as last-minute revision. This is last-minute panic, and what we should've been doing, and what I recommend you do if you are ever in this situation, about to sit an exam, is practise mindfulness and meditation, not try to figure out what questions will appear, or frantically go through battered revision cards. The most important feeling that should be present before an exam is calmness. I was very evidently a hard worker at university, and so a lot of the "last-minute revision" questions were directed at me. I felt my tummy flip and I simply couldn't cope with what was going on around me.

I decided to move away from my peers and find out what was really going on with my exam seat. I found an invigilator, and in classic Onyinye fashion, pointed out that I felt that there was some confusion about my seat. The conversation had the "I would like to speak to the manager" tone. I took my phone out to show them the email I had been sent confirming my attendance at Kensington Olympia. With this in mind, why did the seat allocation notice state that I should be in Waterloo? It turned out that the university admin team had, it seemed to me, made a mistake. I was meant to be at Waterloo because I had extra time. KCL had a policy of separating extra-time students as they recognized that the manic Olympia environment would not enable us to give our exams our very best shot. No one had informed me of this policy, and as I hadn't known about it, I wasn't in a position to ask beforehand. Though I do have to say, to King's credit, it never happened again.

My heart broke...again. I don't like to wallow in problems, and can proudly say that in situations like this, once I've had 5 minutes to cry, I quickly come up with a range of solutions. In this case, however, the situation was totally out of my hands. I found this quite uncomfortable. I had 30 minutes until the start of my exam. The invigilator suggested that I make the 45-minute journey to the Waterloo campus. Instinctively I knew that this was an unrealistic idea. In reality, the journey would have taken me over an hour because the trains from Kensington Olympia run on the most irregular schedule Transport for London has to offer – and this is no exaggeration. The invigilator made a call to the Waterloo campus to notify them of the university admin confusion, but I was given the short straw and told that if I didn't sit the exam at Kensington Olympia, with no extra time or the support I was entitled to, my mark would be an automatic fail and I would have to re-sit in the summer with a mark cap of 40 (the lowest pass mark). Essentially, I was given no choice but to sit the exam there and then. I do understand that mistakes and confusion happen and I am not including this story to allocate blame, but to show that there are a lot of things that can go wrong if you're dyslexic, even when you have good relations with your university and overall a very positive experience of studying there.

A makeshift desk was found for me at the back of the hall. At this point I was already running five minutes behind everyone else because of all the phone calls. Tears were streaming down my face as I dragged my feet to the back of the hall. I was given the exam paper on stark white paper. At this point I was fighting against the symptoms of dyslexia and delirium as the words moved around on the page. I can cope with moving words on most days, but having to deal with it during what was an adult spelling, punctuation and grammar test felt particularly gruelling. I had to get myself together as I was determined not to fail my first exam at university.

In that moment, I knew that the strength of my character was being tested, so I plucked up all the courage I had in me to complete the exam to the best of my ability. I had no extra time, no yellow paper, and no rest breaks – these are the essential comforts and supports I had been used to, that enabled me to reach my academic potential, and, in an instant, they had been stripped away from me. I am oddly grateful for the experience, though, because it was the one occasion where I could see what life must be like for those living with undiagnosed dyslexia. It was awful. The experience has made me even more passionate about raising awareness about dyslexia.

I completed the exam in time, with blisters on my fingers from holding the pen so hard. There were beads of sweat above my brow. I looked like I had just fought in a war. My classmates and I went to the pub across the road from the exam hall. They ordered a bottle of champagne to celebrate completing their first exam; I ordered a sour orange juice. The tangy taste was symbolic of the bittersweet moment I was in. I had just completed my first exam and the likelihood that the grade would be a fail was remarkably high. I was both angry and upset. How could this have happened? The truth is that universities and any large institutions make admin mistakes like this sometimes – they have a lot of students and timetables to manage! The reason I have written about this is because I do wonder whether they realize what the implications of these confusions could be. And if we can share this kind of knowledge more widely, perhaps things will get better as everyone becomes more aware.

I was too afraid to deal with the matter, and decided that I would wait until I received my results before I considered challenging the university. The results were released quickly – I had achieved 59.5, half a mark short of achieving a 2:1. I was initially proud... and then I remembered the conditions that I had sat the exam in, and I was fuming. I fired off an email to my personal tutor and advisor from Disability Support. They were both horrified to hear about what I had gone through, and really supportive, but because I had already sat the exam, we discovered that any further attempt would be capped at the lowest pass mark, 40. I was damned if I did anything and damned if I didn't. I understand that universities need to have to policies and procedures, but a lot of it in my opinion is bureaucratic. And many a time, in my view, the policies and procedures don't help; they merely hinder.

The exams office didn't seem to understand my point of view and didn't seem very apologetic about the confusion with the locations…in fact, as I recall, one staff member suggested that I should be pleased with my result. They were probably trying to comfort me, but I felt insulted by the comment because that result wasn't my best. The whole point of the extra exam conditions was so that I could maximize my potential. Knowing what I know now, I would probably have appealed the exam result, on the grounds that I was not happy with my grade, on the principle that I had been denied an opportunity to do my best. I was able to take comfort from the fact that I did achieve a 2:1 overall in the Study Skills module after the submission of my essay, though, which pulled up my overall mark. If you are in a similar situation you will need to decide what is best for you, too.

Every other exam I sat while at university after this was held at the KCL Waterloo campus. I must say that the invigilators there made every exam experience thoroughly enjoyable. I was given extra time, they made note of my request to have a window seat (I don't like sitting in the aisle of an exam room, as it makes me feel claustrophobic). I was given rest breaks – being an Arts and Humanities student meant that there were times when I had 4+ hour exams due to the additional extra time. I was even allowed to bring light snacks into the exam room. The Waterloo campus invigilators had a habit or way of making us feel like we were not taking an exam. It was incredible. Exam season became my favourite part of the academic year. I had an easy commute to the exam location – one 45-minute bus journey, to be exact. I practised meditation in the bathroom before every exam. I received all my examination resources on coloured paper, and I looked forward to a cheeky Nando's to celebrate getting to the end of the exam paper. When KCL got things right, they got things really right. I achieved some of my best ever marks in exams while at university.

166 | Dyslexia and Me

Now before anyone takes an exam, they must
be taught the content. Experiencing university
teaching styles as a dyslexic person was...
interesting. My undergraduate degree was taught
by staff who came from traditional backgrounds. In
my first term, I did a lot of copying notes from the
board to my bright yellow Word document. This
was hard, especially when all the PowerPoint slide
backgrounds were a bright white (in some cases,
a light blue background with blue text). Visually
it was a mess for me. When I tried to explain the
visual issues I was experiencing to some lecturers,
while they were intrigued and tried hard to support
me, they simply didn't understand dyslexia. It was
clear that there was little to no neurodivergence
training for staff. This is something that needs to
change, and it's not just limited to the university
environment. All educational institutions and
workplaces should have their staff adequately
trained on neurodiversity matters.

I couldn't deliver neurodiversity training, but I
could become a student rep and ignite some sort
of change, so that is what I did. In the middle of my
first term, I was successfully voted in as the first

year rep, and I shared my ideas on what inclusive learning looked like. These included giving the students worksheets to make the lectures more interactive, trips, where possible, seminars, easily accessible office hours and time with students in the cohorts above ours because there's nothing better than learning from someone who has recently had your experience. I developed a great relationship with the Theology and Religious Studies head of department, who was willing to both listen and to learn. I cannot stress the importance of building positive relationships with the teaching staff while at university. If in doubt, just ask. Don't struggle silently.

The first big change the head of department made was to increase the amount of experiential learning we all had. We went on the most incredible trips to various religious sites. The head and the other lecturers made an effort to help us to physically see what we were reading about. They provided us with worksheets that we needed to fill in rather than copy from the board. This meant that my mind was always being positively stimulated. They included film in some of the lectures. Their use of multimedia was fantastic. All these changes were great for my dyslexic mind, and it taught me something new about myself. I realized that I had several different learning styles and that I need to change my learning methods frequently in order to effectively process the information being given to me.

Here is an overview of the four learning style types:

- Visual: Visual leaners retain information when it's presented to them in a graphic depiction. Using arrows, charts, diagrams, symbols and colour can help a visual learner thrive.

- Auditory: Auditory learners prefer to listen to information that is being presented to them vocally. The use of audiobooks and podcasts, as well as simply reading the necessary information out loud to themselves, can help auditory learners engage and retain content.

- Read/write: A read/write learner likes to focus on the written word. They learn best when information is provided to them via worksheets and presentations. Retention takes place when this type of learner takes notes. They may have to take the notes down several times before the information sticks.

- Kinaesthetic: A kinaesthetic learner is a physical learner. They like to be hands-on and will retain information when given the opportunity to role-play or get stuck into an activity related to the subject.[1]

Contrary to popular belief, you can have more than one type of learning style. I went through school thinking that I was only a read/write learner. However, the changes in my lecturers' teaching styles opened my mind and helped me see that I retained information through different mediums. The important thing for me is that I don't get bored. I am aware that this isn't the case for all dyslexic people, but it's important that we all know the ways in which we learn and retain information best.

You may be wondering how you could find out your learning style. It's fairly easy to discover in today's day and age – I did a series of free "learning style" tests online and compared the results. If you have a full assessment with an educational psychologist, they will also give you details on how you might learn best. Knowing what works best for me when learning transformed my university experience.

Where I mostly struggled in my undergraduate years was with reading. The amount of reading was unbelievable. This was to be expected in an Arts and Humanities degree, but I had truly never seen reading lists so long. I had eight modules to read for, each with their own demands. I'm a self-confessed goody two-shoes student, so if you gave me a list with extra reading, I did it. My now dearest friend and university mentor (who I'll refer to as Bubbles, because she truly is the bubbliest person I know) quickly put a stop to me doing the extra reading because, as she said, "Literally no one does it".

Bubbles was the perfect university student and a great example to me. She always handed her work in on time, was superb at referencing and was well read. If she believed that no one did the extra reading, then truly, no one did. It does lead me to question **why** universities dump so much workload on students. Completing the International Baccalaureate (IB) taught me how to manage high volumes of work, but there was a distinct difference between the IB workload and university workload. Every task I was asked to do for my IB was necessary, but even when I did the extra reading at university, it didn't add anything but copious amounts of stress to my day. The lecturers never asked about it, and to be honest, when I included extra readings in my essays, I didn't see drastic changes in my marks.

Dyslexic people can be very literal, and when given instructions, we tend to follow exactly what we've been told. I was literally doing everything that we were told to do, and Bubbles could see me burning out. If she hadn't stepped in, I do wonder what would have happened to me. Universities ought to rethink the amounts and relevance of the work that is being set. At the end of the day, we should leave university equipped with the skills to join the working world. Having been in the working world for a number of years now, I can, hand on heart, say that there has been, and probably will never be, a time when I will have to complete such vast amounts of reading.

The intervention of my friend Bubbles is something that I will be eternally grateful for. It made me aware of the importance of friendships while at university. I spent a lot of my first term feeling isolated, which only made matters worse. I urge you to find friends who are doing the same course as you. Don't be afraid to ask those in the cohorts above you for advice – it is likely that they have had your experience and they will be honest with you.

Once I had a good gauge on just how much reading was necessary, I had time to get involved with other things. I got involved with the wider university community, taking major leadership roles in the King's Think Tank (the largest student-led think tank in Europe) and the Theological and Religious Studies (TRS) Society. I remember what Mr Honourable had taught me, which is that there was more to life than academia. By doing things outside of the library, I was able to see the benefits of dyslexia in the real world. This was a huge confidence booster for me.

Seeing how dyslexia could help rather than hinder me allowed me to love myself. I was (and still am) a creative leader. What I mean by this is that I am constantly thinking outside of the box. I attribute my creativity to my dyslexia…I see the world differently to everyone else. People see my difference in the way that I do things. If I had to organize an event, I would ask myself what we could do to make the event a real showstopper. I ended up leading and hosting an event for the King's Think Tank, after hours, at the Old Bailey – Britain's Central Criminal Court.

When I was president of the TRS Society and had to get vital feedback from students, I discovered different ways in which we could communicate with them. In my year as president, the Theology and Religious Studies department had its highest response rate ever from students. My dyslexia forced me to get organized. It encouraged me to communicate via different mediums. It made me bold – after all, what did I really have to lose? KCL recognized my talents, and, in 2018 I was awarded the inaugural KCL Student of the Year. While I believe that awards do not define who you are, they do help you recognize your value.

I really grew into myself in my undergraduate years. I began to appreciate the power of my mind as well as understanding that my diverse thinking is what helps me to achieve great things. Being in educational spaces that are neurotypical can be exhausting, but once you discover what works best for you, you will love the process of being educated. I loved it so much that I stayed at KCL to complete another degree.

The key takeaways from my undergraduate degree and the advice I would give to all neurodivergent university students are:

1. Familiarize yourself with your university's disability department. Once you know which university you'll be attending, get in touch with them **before** term starts. Don't be afraid to schedule a meeting to meet with a support staff member.

2. Find out what additional support is on offer. For example, at KCL students who have additional needs sit their exams in an environment where

individual needs can be better managed than in a large exam hall, as shown in the experience I had – once I realized this was available!

3. Stay in touch with your personal tutor. Show up to meetings, email them and ask for help when needed. My personal tutor was always supportive of my needs because we had a good working relationship.

4. Have fun! Get involved with everything that the university has to offer – your neurodivergence should not hold you back.

Notes

1. Winton, A. (2018) *Fun Games and Activities for Children with Dyslexia: How to Learn Smarter with a Dyslexic Brain*. London: Jessica Kingsley Publishers.

Chapter 8

The BA to MA Transition

The last few months of my final undergraduate year were riddled with stress and anxiety. I wasn't sure what life beyond university would look like. I had spent all my time as a member of an institution, and the thought of venturing outside the four walls of a classroom was terrifying. I attended several careers exhibitions as well as postgraduate open days, but I still couldn't decide what to do next. It seemed as though everyone got a graduate job once they finished their undergraduate degree. I distinctly remember having conversations with alumni who had gone off to become civil servants or consultants in professional services – these professions seemed popular in the KCL alumni community. I thought

178 | Dyslexia and Me

that I should do the same as my fellow alumni, and in the process, I suffered 39 graduate job rejections.

If there was ever a time in my life when I had experienced the full force of humility, it was then. I was told "no", not once, not twice...but a grand total of 39 times. It came as even more of a shock to me because despite all my hard work, awards and accolades, it seemed that I just wasn't good enough for the corporate world. On reflection, I can see that many of the jobs I applied for weren't the right fit for me, but I think it's fair to say that many of the entry exams for these jobs weren't neurodivergent-friendly.

Graduate entry scheme exams are reminiscent of the 11+ exams. They have very little to do with intelligence; instead it's all about the amount of practice you put in. Past papers were absolute king...and they came at a hefty cost. I paid £75 to gain access to a graduate entry scheme exam question bank. There were a lot of verbal and non-verbal reasoning as well as audit-style maths questions. These were laid out in the form of long, font size 9, Arial paragraphs. The expectation was that the candidate would read, analyze, and then correctly solve whatever problem they had put to them. There were also several spelling, punctuation and grammar-type exercises that were presented as mock emails. Candidates had to correct and complete these emails under timed pressure. The entire experience was, in my view, unnecessary, as the tests almost never assessed candidates on the skills they needed to be good at the job on offer.

I had applied for roles in either Risk Advisory or Communications. There was no maths. In fact, when I did finally get a job offer (from a "Big Four" professional services firm), I was told that I wouldn't even have to use Excel in my role. It did make me wonder why I had been subjected to the horrors of audit-style percentage increase and decrease questions. I also pondered why there had been a need to examine my non-verbal and verbal reasoning skills – my 11+ days were, quite literally, 11 years behind me at this point. The assessment methods seemed to me both dated and inaccessible.

There are many reasons why the assessment methods lack inclusivity. For starters, the affordability of past paper questions is borderline non-existent. You either have £75+ to spare or you have to go into the graduate entry scheme exam process blindly. I scrimped and saved to be able to afford access to a question bank, but this may not be an option for others. The other issue is the amount of time needed to prepare for these tests. If a student has a part-time job to help them afford university life, they will have a lot less time to prepare for the graduate entry scheme test. The unspoken reliance on candidates being able to, first, afford these past papers and, second, have enough "free time" to prepare for these exams cuts the chances of success for those from low socioeconomic backgrounds.

My main gripe with the lack of accessibility is with **how** these exams are run. I'll start with timings... some companies did not allow me to have extra time for the exams. My brain (and many other neurodivergent brains) processes information at a much slower rate than what is considered "normal". This doesn't mean that I can't do the exams; it just means I need a little more time. Extra time levels the playing field and gives me an equitable chance of passing an exam. It seems that certain companies don't appreciate this, and use not completing an exam within the allocated time slots as a form of lowering applicant numbers.

The other issue is the lack of special educational needs provision. At every in-person assessment I attended I was handed an exam paper printed on wintery white paper. The sentiment to offer support was often there with the option to notify the HR office of any needs via an Equalities Act form, but many a time, the action needed to support me never took place. Sentiment is nice, but the truth is that sentiment alone isn't good enough. I began to feel that many of these corporate organizations did not really care about neurodivergent people like me. Satisfying the needs of neurodivergent people seemed to be a tick box exercise in the working world. This forced me to think about whether I really wanted to enter the corporate world of work at all.

One evening, as I was sorting through my paperwork, I came across my Online Education course certificate from Tsinghua University, Beijing. At the end of my second year at university, I was awarded two scholarships that enabled me to spend a summer exchange semester studying in China. I achieved one of the highest marks in my cohort, and my time in China showed me that I had a real affinity with the study of education.

I was offered another scholarship to complete a postgraduate degree there, but I politely declined the offer because I felt that long-term study in China would not work for me due to my dyslexia. While I had the most incredible time, I ended up working the longest hours of my academic life. This wasn't healthy. I lived on 4 hours' sleep, had no access to assistive technology (it was blocked), and spent more time explaining dyslexia to my lecturers than I did asking them questions about the course I was taking. I was mature enough to know that while it seemed like a wonderful opportunity, in reality, it would have been a disaster for me.

Before I go any further, it's important that I discuss the magic that is assistive technology and where you will be able to find it on various devices. Let's start with software features that won't cost you any more than what you've already paid for in a subscription.

- Read Aloud: This feature reads all or part of your document. You can use Read Aloud on its own or within Immersive Reader for Word in Windows and MacOS. It is especially important for dyslexic people because we often miss out words in a sentence and recognize this. The Read Aloud feature helps you spot your mistakes by, quite literally, reading them to you.

- Immersive Reader: This set of tools helps improve reading fluency and comprehension, and includes:[1]

  - Column-width changes that can help you change line length to improve your focus and comprehension.

  - Page colour changes that can help make text easy to scan, thus minimizing eye strain (my pages are permanently set to background colour shade #FFE312).

- Line focus changes can help to remove distractions so that you can move through a document line by line. You can adjust the focus to put one, three or five lines in view at a time.

- Text spacing enables you to increase the spacing between words, characters and lines (I **always** write with 1.5cm line spacing).[2]

• Speak: This function reads text that you've selected. Please note that this feature is only available for Windows.

• Narrator: This is the Windows screen reader app that reads your dialog boxes, buttons and other user interfaces as well as the text.[3]

A notable assistive software package and an all-time favourite in the dyslexia community is Dragon NaturallySpeaking, also known as Dragon for PC, or DNS. It is a speech recognition software package that has voice recognition in dictation with speech transcribed as written text, recognition of spoken commands and text to speech (speaking the text content of a document).

Hardware can also be massively useful. If I were to create a dyslexia goodie bag, it would include the following:

- A Dictaphone: This somewhat aged piece of hardware is a must-have for every dyslexic because it enables you to record lectures, meetings and classes. This means that you can play these sessions back in your own time and take note of the important stuff without the pressure of having to retain everything in your head.

- A C-Pen Reader: This nifty piece of technology is a total life-saver on the days when reading on paper is giving you too much of a headache. To use the pen effectively, you simply scan the line of the text you are trying to read, and it will read it aloud in a human-sounding voice.

- Earplugs: For moments when you just need a bit of silence to write or to simply think. Noise can be hugely distracting for dyslexic people, and can cause us to lose focus.

My time at Tsinghua University showed me one very important thing – I had mastered the art of studying and had an unending passion for education. I was already running my then nine-year-old tuition business. I singlehandedly built the Enrich Learning website with plans to lead the online education industry in the UK. Applying to undertake a postgraduate degree in Education seemed like a no-brainer. I deferred my entry to the "Big Four" firm by a year and decided to live out my dream of becoming a leading expert in Education.

I only submitted one postgraduate degree application. I'll be honest – the main reason for this was cost. For many UK universities you need to pay for your postgraduate degree applications, which are expensive, and funding for these applications is limited. I didn't have access to funds that would support more than one attempt. My second reason was that I was comfortable at King's College London (KCL). While I'm a big believer of stepping out of your comfort zone, I also think it's important to know your limits. Despite the disaster that was my inaugural university exam, KCL had helped me manage my dyslexia really well. I didn't want to run the risk of going to a new institution that may not have been able to make sufficient provisions for me. After a very welcoming meeting with the programme director for the Education, Policy and Society MA at KCL, I decided to submit an application, and hoped for the best.

While I prepared for life as a postgraduate, I also officially began my career as an entrepreneur. I formally registered my company after a gentle push from one of my business mentors and surrogate big sisters. I had a vision of building an EdTech while learning all that I needed to know about Education via my postgraduate degree. I made that vision a reality by studying in various cafes and libraries across London during the day, and then building my business late at night (many a time in the early hours of the morning too). My course was slightly unusual in that all my classes were in the evening to allow those who had day jobs the opportunity to attend. It was the perfect set-up for me.

I thoroughly enjoyed my postgraduate year of study. It was my favourite year in education. I had learnt what worked best for me, and was lucky enough to be taught by lecturers who understood the importance of inclusivity in the classroom. Many of my lecturers had come from a school teaching background and had dealt with various forms of neurodivergence in the past. This meant that my request to have PowerPoint slides with a yellow background were understood and executed. In actual fact, yellow PowerPoint slides became department standard while I was studying there. I felt a strong sense of belonging in the department, and this gave me the strength and ability to thrive.

Academically, I achieved my highest marks in my postgraduate year. At this point in my life, I was technically savvy, meaning that I knew what software features helped me read and write efficiently. I absolutely loved what I was doing. I was happy. I didn't realize just how much of a role mental health plays when studying until I was in the thick of my MA studies. Happiness got me through the difficult times. I fell quite ill with COVID-19 halfway through my year of study. While I could barely make it up the stairs without huffing and puffing, I was happy to fight extreme fatigue to write my essays and read my papers.

The COVID-19 pandemic forced an unforeseen shift in education that affected both neurotypical and neurodivergent people. For me, personally, the shift enriched my postgraduate experience. Everything went digital, which meant that I no longer had to spend time and money increasing my carbon footprint, copying my reading papers onto yellow paper. Instead, I could change the background shade on an electronic device. I saved a lot of storage on my phone as I didn't need to record my lecturers independently. All lectures were recorded and uploaded to the university's e-learning platform. I could play back the lecturers' teachings as and when I wanted. I was given a lot more one-on-one teaching time. There was no need to factor in travel time, meaning that my lecturers and I had a lot more flexibility to meet virtually – which was invaluable.

Of course, I missed the buzz of being in a seminar room and meeting other students, but I believe that the overall quality of teaching improved. I know that this has not been the case for everyone who was thrown into the world of virtual learning, but I am sharing my positive experiences with the hopes that those who come across them can see the value in remote learning when executed well.

Here are a few tips that helped me master the tricks of the e-learning trade:

1. Allow your email app to become your favourite mode of communication. Remote learning means that you cannot just pop into your lecturer's office to ask a quick question, but you can drop them a line and they will get back to you. Don't be afraid to email your lecturer again if you have heard nothing from them after a reasonable amount of time. I found email to be better than the face-to-face meetings because this form of communication made it easier to go back and cross-check what had been said rather than relying on my memory or badly taken notes.

2. Don't just rely on recordings – attend the live class. I know I have quite publicly declared my love for recorded classes, but I didn't depend

on them. I attended every live virtual session and was amazed by how similar it was to the face-to-face experience. In a live session you can ask questions and get real-time answers in the same way that you would in a face-to-face classroom. Recordings are a bonus and shouldn't be treated as the main source of the class.

3. Use tracked changes when getting feedback on drafts. Tracked changes enabled me to actually see how I could have improved my writing. When your lecturer or study buddy makes adaptations or suggestions to your work, tracked changes will, rather efficiently, show the exact change that was made. Prior to the e-learning phenomenon, feedback on my writing was often collected in the form of scribbled down notes that I wrote in haste. It was hard for me to see what changes I needed to make to improve my work until I actively encouraged those who worked with me to use tracked changes.

I went on to achieve a Merit (annoyingly my mark was 69, one mark off a distinction) in my postgraduate degree. I did, however, achieve a distinction in my research-based dissertation. Apart from this book you're reading right now, my postgraduate dissertation is my proudest piece of work to date. It even found itself on a desk in Number 10 Downing Street. My research on the "Urban Digital Divide and Parental Engagement in Education" was highly commended and, most importantly to me, informed the strategic moves I made to grow my business, which is now helping children access education across the world.

My academic life came to an end on a high, with me, a dyslexic student, being given an award as one of 2020's top 10 Black Students in the UK. Rare Recruitment, in partnership with the Universities of Oxford and Cambridge, gave this award to me. To be recognized in such a prestigious way is one of the greatest honours of my life. It's especially important to me because it proved that everyone, including myself, had been wrong about my limits. It made me know that I am, in fact, audaciously limitless in my pursuits. My positive outlook on everything, even in trying times, helped me build strength, courage and confidence. I dared to be proudly different, with tremendous success.

As I bring this book to a close, I want to remind you of why I decided to share my story. I have shared my story because the dyslexia community lacked (and still lacks) diversity. I want to lead from the front and, quite literally, change the narrative. I have opened myself up in a way that I have never done before, and in the process exposed my vulnerabilities. I have pushed myself beyond measure. Throughout this book I have noted that a general misconception is that dyslexic people cannot read and or write well. I hope you can see that this is simply not true. This book is evidence that dyslexic people **can** read and write; the only difference is the way in which they execute the task. That difference, along with all the other differences I have mentioned, should not only be acknowledged; **they should be celebrated**.

Notes

1. Microsoft Support (no date) 'Listen to your Word documents.' Available at https://support.microsoft.com/en-us/office/listen-to-your-word-documents-5a2de7f3-1ef4-4795-b24e-64fc2731b001, accessed on 11 October 2021.

2. Microsoft Support (no date) 'Learning tools in Word.' Available at https://support.microsoft.com/en-us/office/learning-tools-in-word-a857949f-c91e-4c97-977c-a4efcaf9b3c1, accessed on 11 October 2021.

3. Microsoft Support (no date) 'Listen to your Word documents.' Available at https://support.microsoft.com/en-us/office/listen-to-your-word-documents-5a2de7f3-1ef4-4795-b24e-64fc2731b001, accessed on 11 October 2021.

Epilogue

If there is only one thing that you take away after reading this book, let it be that representation matters. Eleven-year-old me had no dyslexic person she could relate to. There was no one in the public eye who looked like me and who openly discussed their dyslexia. There was no one talking about neurodivergence freely in my community. There was no one I could consider my role model and **genuinely** look up to. I soon realized that I needed to use my gifts to develop my character in a way that would encourage others (and myself) to look up to me. There is power in being your own role model; I just wish I had known this sooner. This book is my attempt at being the representation that 11-year-old me, and so many people across the world, so desperately need.

I have written this book in a bid to inspire you. I have wholeheartedly worn my heart on my sleeve and shared my highest highs and my lowest lows. I urge you, however, not to compare yourself to me directly or in unhelpful ways. Instead, take my unique and positive story and use it to authentically create your own unique positive story. Learn from my mistakes, use the tips I have given you to create your own methods, and be unapologetically you. In a world where human beings have been, in many ways, forced to be the same, let this book remind you to celebrate and showcase your difference.

To my dyslexic friends, if you've made it this far, well done! Make sure you raise a glass and embrace the gifts of neurodivergence.

Resources

Dyslexia websites

British Dyslexia Association
www.bdadyslexia.org.uk

0333 405 4555

Helen Arkell – Provides assessments and advice for dyslexics
www.helenarkell.org.uk

01252 749 400

Dyslexia Scotland
www.dyslexiascotland.org.uk

0344 800 84 84

Dyslexia Assessments London – An educational psychologist providing assessments for young people and adults
www.dyslexia-london.com
079 413 41327

Cursive Writing – Handwriting worksheets
www.cursivewriting.org

Spellzone – Useful for word pattern lists (e.g., words ending 'cian')
www.spellzone.com
0333 990 0132

WordHippo spelling resources – Useful for word pattern lists
www.wordhippo.com

Free online printable times tables cards
www.guruparents.com

Olivia Hickmott – The Learning Coach and Expert in Visualization
https://olivehickmott.wordpress.com/empowering-learning
07970 854 388

Made By Dyslexia
https://www.madebydyslexia.org

Mental health organizations

World Federation for Mental Health
https://wfmh.global

Samaritans
www.samaritans.org
08457 90 90 90

YoungMinds
www.youngminds.org.uk

Anxiety UK – Advice and support for people living with anxiety
anxietyuk.org.uk
03444 775 774 (helpline)
07537 416 905 (text)

Beat – Under 18s helpline, webchat and online support groups for people with eating disorders, such as anorexia and bulimia
www.beateatingdisorders.co.uk

0808 801 0711 (youthline)
0808 801 0811 (studentline)

**Campaign Against Living Miserably (CALM) –
Provides listening services, information and
support for anyone who needs to talk, including a
web chat**
0800 58 58 58
www.thecalmzone.net

**Childline – Support for children and young people
in the UK, including a free helpline and 1-2-1 online
chats with counsellors**
0800 1111
www.childline.org.uk

**OCD Youth – Youth Support for young people with
obsessive-compulsive disorder (OCD)**
www.ocdyouth.org

**On My Mind – Information for young people to
make informed choices about their mental health
and wellbeing**
www.annafreud.org/on-my-mind

Anti-bullying organizations

https://anti-bullyingalliance.org.uk – Anti-bullying Alliance

Kidscape.org.uk – Help with bullying

Respectme.org.uk – Scotland's anti-bullying service

Place2BE – leading UK provider of school-based mental health services

www.place2be.org.uk

020 7923 5500

The Cybersmile Foundation

www.cybersmile.org

0808 800 2222

National Bullying Helpline

https://www.nationalbullyinghelpline.co.uk

National Society for the Prevention of Cruelty to Children (NSPCC)

www.nspcc.org.uk

0800 800 5000 (for adults concerned about a child)

0800 1111 (18 or under – Childline helpline)

Index

accommodations
    coloured paper and overlays
        114–17, 150, 165
    time allowances 58–9,
        124–5, 156
activities (extra-curricular)
    37–9, 51–2, 56–8, 86,
    133–5, 145, 172
    and burnout 86, 171
anxiety 86, 171, 157–60, 177
    and irritable bowel syndrome
        (IBS) 120, 124, 130–1, 157
apps and software support
    85, 182–5, 190
Arnett, A.B. 42
assessments for dyslexia
    63–6, 89–93
    in adulthood 150–4
assistive technologies 182–6
auditory learners 168

BBC News 63–4
boredom 38
Branson, Richard 10–11, 93

British Dyslexia Association
    (BDA) 29–30, 63, 65, 69
bullying 114–21, 125–33
    consequences of 120–1, 130–1
burnout 86, 171

camouflaging techniques 24, 83
change 80–1
China, studying in 181–2
choice and education 63, 106
Christ's Hospital school
    8, 60–2, 69, 71–97
coloured filters/overlays
    114–17, 150, 165
comprehensive school systems
    access to dyslexia
        support 63–8
    vs. private schools
        61–4, 68, 102–4
concentration abilities 55
confidence-building measures
    32–3, 37–9, 42–3
COVID-19 188–9
C-Pen Readers 185

cultural competence 43–4
cultural factors 38–45
    and learning differences
        9, 29, 43, 90–4
curiosity 38

daily routines and
    schedules 52–7
debating skills 133–4
Department of Education 63–4
diagnosis of dyslexia 8
    assessments for 63–6,
        89–93, 150–4
    costs of 65
    and gender 42–3
    in adulthood 150–4
    and "labelling" concerns
        29–30
    not knowing about 17–18,
        42–3, 51, 58–9, 63–9, 162
    screening for 66–8, 154
Dictaphones 185
"difference" 94–6
    see also learning differences
Dragon NaturallySpeaking
    (Dragon for PCs) 184–5
Driver Youth Trust 28
dyslexia
    family history of 17–20
    key challenges of 55
    masking techniques 24, 85, 88
    positive aspects of 11,
        93, 95–6, 195–6
    resources for 33
    role models/ambassadors
        10–11, 93–5, 195–6
    science of 19–20
    and self-blame 27–8, 42–3

suggestions for improving
    understanding 94–6
tips for primary years 32–3
undiagnosed 17–18, 42–3,
    51, 58–9, 63–9, 162
visual symptoms 114–20, 166
dyslexia assessments
    63–6, 89–93, 150–4
    in adulthood 150–4
    costs of 65, 152–4
dyslexia screening 66–8, 154

earplugs 185–6
educational systems
    online services 109–11
    state vs. private schools
        61–4, 68, 102–4
eidetic memory 23–4
Einstein, Albert 10–11, 93–4
11+ exams 57–9, 69
email apps 190
employment applications 177–81
empowerment 41–2,
    99–100, 107–11
Enrich Learning 8, 59, 99–111
entrepreneurship 96–7,
    99–111, 145
equity vs. equality 45–7, 62, 96
exams
    importance of early
        experiences 59, 106–7
    key problems with 180–1
    managing well 165–6
    time allowances 58–9,
        124–5, 159–60, 165
    when things go wrong 156–64
    see also graduate job
        applications

experiential learning 167–8
extra-curricular activities
    37–9, 51–2, 54, 56–8,
    86, 133–5, 145, 172

families
    history of dyslexia 17–20
    from immigrant
        backgrounds 38–45
    sibling learning differences
        9, 15–17
    siblings and birth order 39–41
    support with spelling 13, 16–18
famous people with
    dyslexia 10–11
#FFE312 (yellow) paper
    114–16, 150
The Fish in the Tree: Why We Are
    Failing Children with Dyslexia
    (Driver Youth Trust) 28
friendships 82, 172
funding for assessments
    65–6, 152–4

gender inequality 45
gender issues
    cultural expectations 39–41
    dyslexia diagnosis and
        support 42–3
genetics and dyslexia 17–20
Goldberg, Whoopi 94
graduate job applications 177–81
grammar and punctuation
    difficulties 24–7

Hodgson, Sharon 64
homework
    difficulties with 9

parental help 16–18, 20–4
hyper-focusing 74–5

Ibbertson, C. 28
Igbo peoples 39–41, 126–7
    and importance of
        education 123
Immersive Reader 183–4
immigrant families 38–9
    and cultural norms 39–45
    see also cultural factors
inequity, see inequality
    45–7, 62–3, 96
"inner critic" 27–8
International Baccalaureate (IB)
    Diploma Programme 137–41
International Dyslexia
    Association 33
intersectionality 44–9
irritable bowel syndrome (IBS)
    120, 124, 130–1, 157

kinaesthetic learners 169
King's College London (KCL) 7
    post-graduate studies 186–93
    undergraduate studies 146–75

"labelling" children 29–30
learning differences
    and cultural taboos 90–4
    and organizational
        skills 55, 57, 72
    recognition of neurodiversity
        28–31, 63–8, 86–96
    vs. "learning difficulties" 90–1
    ways to improve
        understanding 94–6
learning resources 33

learning styles 93, 167–9
linear thinking 79–80

McGowan, J. 23–4
MacOS software features 183
mapping apps 85
map reading skills 22–3,
    76–9, 82, 85, 148–9, 157
masking dyslexia 24, 83, 88
Meares-Irlen syndrome/
    Irlen syndrome 119
media platforms 95–6
memory
    eidetic memory 23–4
    photographic 22–3, 81–2, 83
mental health, importance
    of 188–9
motor coordination issues 72
multi-tasking skills 38, 55
"muscle memory" 81–2, 84, 88–9

Narrator app 184
navigation skills 76–9,
    148–9, 157–8
neurodivergence
    and cultural taboos 90–4
    lack of awareness of 28–31
    and organizational
        skills 55, 57, 72
    recognition of 28–31,
        63–8, 86–96
    role models for 93–5, 195–6
    ways to improve
        understanding 94–6
neuro-linguistic programming
    (NLP) 121–2
New Scientist 23

Nigerian heritage 39–41,
    122–3, 126–7

obsessive thinking 21, 88, 123
    and perfectionism 88, 106, 136
    and rituals 75–7, 85–7
Office for National Statistics 65
Oliver, Jamie 10–11, 93
online education services 109–11
"opara" (eldest child) 39–41
opportunities for learning 37–9
    state vs. private schools
        61–4, 68, 102–4
    see also Enrich Learning
organizational skills 55, 57, 72
    tips for 84–6
overlays/coloured filters
    114–17, 150, 165
Oxford university 144–5

pangrams 115
parental support 16–18,
    20–4, 32–3, 37–43
parents
    acceptance of diagnosis 9–10
    with dyslexia 17–20
    support for 28–31
perfectionism 88, 106, 136
photographic memory
    22–3, 71, 83
positive affirmations 32
positive outlooks 9–10,
    121, 192–3, 196
post-graduate education 177–93
    see graduate jobs 177–81
    research dissertations 192
    and virtual learning 189–91

poverty, and under-served
families 45–6
preparation/planning tips 84–6
primary school experiences
8–9, 13–33
problems with written
work 24–7
spelling difficulties
13–17, 20–4
tips for confidence-
building 32–3
private academic tuition
37–8, 51–2, 57–8
private schooling 57–63
and dyslexia support 61–9
processing styles and speeds
52, 79, 83, 87, 137, 168
prompts and reminders 56–7
punctuation and grammar
difficulties 24–7

race 47–8
see also cultural factors
Rare Recruitment awards 7, 192
Read Aloud 183
reading, importance of 135–6
reading lists 170–1
reading support 31–3, 32–3
assistive technologies 182–6
use of overlays 114–17,
150, 165
recording lectures/
lessons 185, 191–2
re-framing techniques 121–2
rituals 75–7, 85–7
role models, importance
of 93–5, 195–6
routines and schedules 52–7

schoolbag packing 75, 77, 85–6
schools
access to dyslexia
support 63–8
state vs. private 61–4,
68, 102–4
see also primary school
experiences; secondary
education
school uniforms 71–2
scotopic sensitivity
syndrome (SSS) 119
screening for dyslexia 66–8, 154
Searleman, A. 23
secondary education 71–97,
102–4, 113–41
getting the best from 135–7
initial experiences 71–84
and International
Baccalaureate (IB) Diploma
Programme 137–41
peer pressures and
bullying 114–35
planning tips 84–7
recognition of dyslexia 87–96
support measures 113–19,
121–2, 124–6, 132–5
seeking help 86
self-blame feelings 27–8, 42–3
self-esteem
confidence-building measures
32–3, 37–9, 42–3
see also empowerment
siblings
and birth order 39–41
learning abilities 9, 15–17
sleep 54, 56
social class 45–7

social media use 126–8
socioeconomic factors 44–7
   and inequity 45–6, 62–3, 96
software support
   measures 182–5
spelling difficulties 13–17, 20–4
   help for 20–4
state school systems
   access to dyslexia
      support 63–8
   vs. private schools
      61–4, 68, 102–4
support measures, for
   parents 28–31

teacher training (learning
   differences) 27–8
tests
   and timekeeping 52–3
   see also exams
thinking patterns
   creative/outside the
      box styles 172–3
   and linear concepts 79–80
   and processing speeds
      52–3, 79, 87, 137
   "wandering minds" 38, 74–5
   see also obsessive thinking
time factors 52–3
   dyslexia diagnosis allowances
      58–9, 124–5, 159–60, 165
   importance of schedules 52–5
time management 55,
   73–4, 79–82
timetables 81–2

transitions, primary to
   secondary school 80–1
tutoring services 100–11

"under-served" families 45–6
undiagnosed dyslexia 17–18,
   42–3, 51, 58–9, 63–9, 162
university education 143–75
   building positive relationships
      167, 173–5
   choice of 143–7
   dyslexia support
      measures 147–56
   managing exams well 165–6
   and outside work 145
   and self-help 154–5
   teaching methods and
      learning styles 166–72
   tips for 174–5
   and virtual learning 189–91
   when things go wrong 156–64

virtual learning 189–91
visualizations 121–2
visual learners 168
visual symptoms of dyslexia
   114–20, 166

"wandering minds" 38, 74–5
whiteboards 75, 118–20
Wilson, Jacqueline 24
Windows software
   features 182–4
Winton, A. 169
writing skills 24–7, 135, 136–7